LANFRANCO FRANZONI

VERONA

108 Colour Plates - 1 Map

Verona. Aerial view.

STORTI EDIZIONI

The Ala of the Amphitheatre.

INTRODUCTION

Verona, according to the attestation of Pliny the Elder, is a Rhaetian and Euganean city. In fact, it rose before the Veneto was included in the Roman system, on a territory where three peoples and three civilizations met; Veneto, Rhaetian, Gallic. More precisely it appears that Verona represents the extreme southern ramification of a Rhaetian infiltration among Veneto populations to the east and Gallic to the West. The most ancient sign of the presence of Rome at Verona and in the Veneto is the route of the Via Postumia, largely realized by Spurius Posthumius Albinus, consul in 148 B.C. But even earlier, between 225 and 221 B.C., Veneti and Cenoman fought on the side of Rome in the war against the Gauls Insubres and Boii. Veneto forces then took part in the 2nd Punic War as allies of Rome against Hannibal's army. We have no monumental evidence of a pre-Roman

Verona, which must have developed on what is now St. Peter's hill, in a point which offered a certain possibility of an easy ford across the river. The official act of birth of the city of Verona as a settlement organized in accordance with the Roman urban criterion is represented by the inscription to be seen on the republican Gate of the Lions, in which are mentioned the **quattuorvirs** who were responsible for the contracts and approved the various installations of the city: walls, gates, sewers (and then the streets). The presence of the **quattuorvirs,** magistrates who governed a Roman municipality, permits the dating of this operation to around the year 49 B.C. when Verona, together with other cities of the Transpadana region, gained Roman citizenship. Right up until the war undertaken by Augustus in 16 B.C. against the Alpine populations, to settle the northern boundaries of Italy, and from the following constitution of the provinces of Rezia and Norico (14 B.C.) Verona was on the line of the northern boundary of Italy, later substituted in this position by the city of Trent. Verona was to enjoy a particularly

The Arena.

happy period under the empire of Claudius (41 - 54 A.D.) and that of Nero (54 - 68 A.D.) during which its city gates were renewed and it had the courtesy title of **Colonia Augusta,** renewed in 265 by the emperor Gallienus: **Colonia Augusta Verona Nova Gallieniana.** In the year 265, the hurried and tumultuous erection of a new circle of walls, which replaced the Republican one in brick, by now completely inefficient after a long period of peace, returned Verona to a situation analogous to that of its origins, within a perimeter, corresponding to that of the Republican era, which sacrificed all the enlargement that the city had had outside this exiguous boundary during almost three centuries of industrious prosperity. The 4th Century was for Verona, as for that matter for a great part of the Empire, the period of the assertion of Christianity linked here with the work of the «coloured» Bishop S. Zeno, 8th in the city's series of Bishops, who died in 372. Verona, too, suffered religious controversies, as seems evident from the inscription of Valerius Palladius in 379 A.D., recording the erection of a

Statue in the busiest part of the Forum; it had long lain in the Capitol and was subsequently invested with a religious significance. Open controversies presumably ceased after 394, when the dreams of a pagan restoration of the tyrant Eugenius were dashed and he was conquered by Theodosius in the Battle of the Frigido. After the fall of the Empire, Verona enjoyed a period of prestige during the reign of Theodoric (489 - 526), who chose it as one of his favourite residences, to such a degree that German legend regards the Gothic king as a Veronese; Theodoric of Verona. The same legend even attributes the building of the Arena to him. On the other hand, historical sources credit him with erection of the baths, of a palace, and of an arcade from the city gate to the palace itself. Even the location of these works is no longer known for certain. In fact, what is popularly known as the Castle of Theodoric on the Colle di San Pietro, behind the former Austrian barracks, is actually the remains of a fort, renovated during the brief period of rule by the Visconti family and subsequently used also by the Venetian Republic. In 568 Verona fell under Longobard dominion and was chosen by Alboin as his place of residence. Alboin was killed in Verona in 572, following a plot instigated by his wife Rosamund. The Longobard goldsmith's work of the Miniscalchi Mansion (1906) and in Via Monte Suello (1964) are the best known testimony of this barbaric population in the city. In 774 Verona witnessed the last Longobard resistance, led by Adelchis, against the French of Charles the Great. Verona, according to the orders introduced into Italy by the Franks, became the centre of a county, but thanks to recurring visits of Pippin, who loved to pay it frequent visits, it assumed from time to time the position of capital of the kingdom. An ancient Veronese tradition indicates on the side of the Basilica of S. Zeno the «Sepulchre of Pippin» but it is known that the French king died at Milan in 810 and was buried there. The so-called «Carolingian Renaissance had a sound representative in Verona in the person of Archdeacon Pacificus (d. 846), whose epitaph in the Cathedral attributes to him, among other things, the authorship of 218 codexes which enrich the Capitulary Library. Successive historical vicissitudes which greatly concerned Verona are those regarding the Italian Kingdom and the figure of Berengarius who met death in Verona following a plot in the year 924.

At the beginning of the 12th century, after the period of the government of the Counts, the Commune took shape and juridical status. The first records of the Consuls are to

Castelvecchio. Cangrande

be found in documents of 1136. At this time the present Basilica of S. Zeno was erected; the lunette above the main door shows the **militia** of the Commune around the Patron Saint. In the quarrels between Communes and Empire, Verona was first on the side of the League, then, under the influence of Ezzelino da Romano, sided with the imperials. The policy led the city slowly towards the institution of the Seigniory, first that of Ezzelino, later of the Della Scala family. From 1262 when Mastino was elected **Captain of the People,** till 1387, when Antonio fled by night from Verona, seeking shelter in Venice, the city was practically always under the Scaligers, whose power had official sanction when they were granted the title **Imperial Vicars.**
During the Scaliger period the city was enriched by a noble series of monuments, from the Arches to Castelvecchio with its wonderful bridge, to the fountain in Piazza Erbe. The Della Scala family residence on Piazza dei Signori saw Dante as guest, first of Bartolomeo and later of Cangrande, who aroused the Poet's hopes and admiration with his pro-Imperial politics. Cangrande extended the circle of the city

walls to the south, so far beyond the boundaries of that of the Commune that its enlargement was sufficient to accommodate the development of the city up to the First World War. After the fall of the Scaligers, Verona was subjected to the seigniory of Gian Galeazzo Visconti, from 1387 until his death in 1402.
After a short period under the Carrarese, on June 24, 1405 came the surrender of Verona to Venice. Thus began for the city of the Adige one of the longest periods of political peace in its history, lasting until 1797, when the Republic of the Veneto fell before the thrust of the Napoleonic army. The only interruption was represented by the short imperial dominion, which removed Verona from Venetian authority from 1509 to 1516. During the almost four centuries in which the city formed part of the Venetian Republic the most illustrious and glorious episodes in the history of Italian art took place and Verona participated in equal measure in the definition of the cultural pattern of the Veneto of this long period. Thus, firstly it promoted the diffusion of the elegance of flamboyant Gothic through the personalities of Stefano and Pisanello, and then welcomed the Tuscan appeal for a return to the rigour, through the mediation of Mantegna and Fra' Giocondo. Later, the presence of Sanmicheli released Verona from the repetition of Lombard forms and brought it to enjoy the glorious experience of a Roman monumentality. The work of Michele Sanmicheli, with the building of the mansions in Corso Cavour, with the opening of Corso Porta Nuova and the erection of the gates which end these two important road axes, contributed in a decisive way to determining the urban aspect of modern Verona, developed within the circle of the Veneto walls. During the long period of Venetian domination the city's major economic activities were the **wool industry,** which however declined during the second half of the 16th century, and the **silk industry,** which developed to fill the gap thus created. The happenings which mostly shook the peaceful course of city life were the three disastrous plagues of the years 1511, 1575 and 1630.
After the fall of the «Serenissima» and the overturning of the old structures produced by the Napoleonic disturbance, there was, starting from the year 1814, the Austrian restoration accompanied, especially after 1833, by the ever-increasing characterization of Verona as a military city. The Austrians set about strengthening the city walls of the Venetian era, with more modern military engineering techniques, and enlarged the fortification system with a double series of small fortresses in the surrounding territory; thanks to their elevated location several of these, such as the Sofia, San Leonardo, San Mattia and delle Torricelle, have become prominant landmarks in the landscape of Verona, just as the great barracks dominate the city from the Colle di San Pietro. The Arsenale di Campagnola is also Austrian, with its grounds which for some time have been designated to become a public park. The annexation of the Veneto to Italy in 1886 did not modify this situation and the double barrier of fortifications built around Verona by Austria was maintained in a state of efficiency to combat the danger of an Austrian return. The disastrous flooding of the Adige river in 1882 and the subsequent construction of embankments from 1889 to 1895, changed the aspect of the city of Verona radically, so that instead of a riverside city it became a city intersected by the same river. Verona ceased being a frontier city only after the victory of November 4, 1918. After the war the city began to expand slowly beyond the circle of its walls, within the first bend of the river, that area which took the name of Borgo Trento. Then the vicissitudes between the two wars soon halted development and Verona resumed its function as a garrison city. In the course of the last war it had also the dismal privilege of becoming the clandestine capital of an ephemeral republic. What Verona has done, and how it has been transformed since 1945 is the living history of our times.

4

SAN ZENO

There are no monuments in Verona to testify to the hegemony of the barbaric invaders in the city, although there are many indications, in San Stefano, the Duomo, S. Maria Antica, San Lorenzo and elsewhere, that even at that time the arts were not completely ignored. But it was only with the establishment of the Commune that buildings worthy to stand beside those of Roman Verona were constructed. The church of San Zeno, burnt down by the «infidel», was rebuilt by the archdeacon Pacificus prior to the year 806 and on May 21st, 807, the church whose reconstruction had been ordered by the French king Pippin and Bishop Rotaldus became the sanctuary for the reliquaries of the Holy Bishop, patron saint of Verona, brought there by the two hermits Benignus and Carus who had been expressly called from their monastery on the Baldo, above Malcesine, to perform this sacred duty. In 900 raiding Hungarians razed the church of San Zeno to the ground and spread ruin throughout the city. It was only at the beginning of the 11th century, with the Hungarian invasions safely in the past, and with the realisations of the necessity for the creation of a Commune to protect the future of the citizens, that the present Basilica of San Zeno began to assume its definitive form, flanked by the great Benedictine monastery. The church is situated some way from the Roman city centre, within the bounds of the largest necropolis of the Roman era, which stretched alongside the Via Gallica, linking Verona with Brescia. The new Basilica,

which suffered damage in the earthquake of 1117, must have been almost finished by 1138.

The high belltower (72 metres) was begun in 1045 and completed in 1178.

To the left of the façade rises the **Abbey Tower,** with its interior frescoes repeating the theme of the Wheel of Fortune on the church façade. The tower is all that remains today of the great and powerful Benedictine monastery.

The Basilica of San Zeno with the Tower of the Abbey

San Zeno. Portal.

SAN ZENO · PORCH AND DOOR

The façade of San Zeno offers a vast prospect of Paduan Romanesque sculpture. The circular band enclosing the lunette above the door bears the engraved name of the sculptor Nicolò, also to be found on the Duomo in Ferrara. Simeoni observed that the lunette itself celebrates the founding of the Commune of Verona, with the figure of San Zeno in the centre holding the standard of the city and trampling a defeated devil. Several of the miracles performed by the saint are represented on the band below the lunette. The two architraves which function as imposts supporting the vault of the porch, however, are decorated with representations of the months, grouped in threes.

The marble reliefs to the right of the porch are signed by the same Nicolò and show scenes from the Old Testament; those to the left, with scenes from the Life of Christ, bear the name of the sculptor Guglielmo. The lower reliefs are set apart from the whole in that their subject matter is not religious; to the right is Theodoric hunting, to the left two stages of a duel. These marble reliefs provide a fitting frame for the magnificent **bronze doors,** composed of forty-eight panels, only two of which have secular themes, the two showing antique masks. The left-hand door is the older, mostly executed by the First Master, the right-hand side being more recent and the work of the Second Master, while the four panels lowest on the right, representing stories from the life of San Zeno, are by the Third Master. As can be seen this is not a unified work, but was executed in two stages, before and after the 1117 earthquake.

SAN ZENO. SCULPTURES AT THE SIDES OF THE PORCH

The relief of «Original Sin» placed beside that of the «Kiss of Judas» provides an opportunity for comparing the two sculptors Nicolò and Guglielmo. The first shows a rather coarse, more vigorous style, with consistently large figures, and a mastery of an entire representational repertory, and is thus to be considered in relation to Wiligelmo, the greatest of the Po Valley Romanesque sculptors whose work is to be found on the Duomo in Modena. Guglielmo appears stylistically more fluent, less concerned to concentrate all attention and energy in the figures themselves, but at times breaks his scene up into a more varied architectural space.

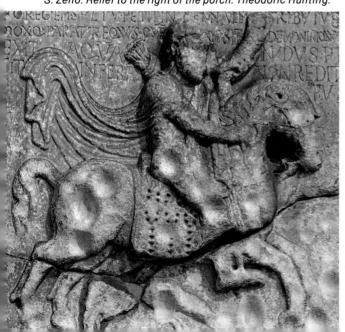

S. Zeno. Relief to the right of the porch: Theodoric Hunting.

S. Zeno. Relief to the left of the porch: Encounter between knights.

San Zeno. Triptych by Andrea Mantegna.

San Zeno. Statue of San Zeno.

SAN ZENO. INTERIOR

The dominant element of the interior of San Zeno is the spaciousness of the central nave, with the linear progress of the coffered «ship's keel» ceiling above. At the end of the third bay the crypt marks the division of the lower church from the upper church or chancel. The crypt, whose generous proportions make it a real underground church, houses the urn containing the remains of the saint, rediscovered in 1838. To the right is the urn of the Three Saints (Lucillus, Lupicinus and Crescentianus), a vigorous example of early 12th century sculpture. Returning to the upper church from the crypt we note the statues of Christ and the Apostles ranged along the balustrade, the work of German sculptors of the early 13th century. The main altar is dominated by the triptych altarpiece painted by Mantegna between 1457 and 1459, the first important Renaissance painting to be seen in Verona. In the small apse to the left is the marble statue of a benign **«San Zeno laughing»,** datable to the beginning of the 14th century. Near the door leading to the sacristy is the statue of San Proculus, signed and dated by Giovanni di Rigino (14th century).

Back on the level of the lower church, beyond the altar of the Madonna Addolorata, we find the door leading to the Cloisters, with the unusual combination of small round arches with ogival.

San Zeno. Interior.

9

SAN BERNARDINO

Renaissance art developed in Verona considerably later than in Florence, as is evidenced by three important churches, San Tommaso Cantuariense, S. Nazaro and S. Bernardino which all display overall Gothic characteristics. Yet in S. Bernardino the simplicity and clear articulation of the façade with its double-pitched crown, and the marble frame of the principal doorway, attenuate the purely Gothic, imposing a rhythm and order of a more classical nature. The somewhat strange ground plan of the church, with the principal nave flanked on the right by a smaller nave into which face all the chapels, is evidently a modification of an original, single-naved plan. The large chapel opening immediately on the right side of the smaller nave, called the Chapel of St. Francis or of the Terziari, was frescoed in 1522 by Nicolò Giolfino with stories from the life of the saint of Assisi, where the influence of Lotto may be discerned, and stories of St. John the Evangelist. The third chapel, despite its paucity of works of artistic interest, is to be remembered in connexion with the Canossa family; here were buried, among others, Girolamo Canossa and his wife Creusa Costanzi. Girolamo created a magnificent collection of archeological and artistic treasures in his palace near the Castelvecchio, in the second half of the 16th century. The fourth chapel, called the Chapel of St. Anthony or of the Medici, contains what little remains today of the frescoes painted by Domenico Morone in 1511. The artist is however also represented, together with his son Francesco, in the library of the monastery where his frescoes, fortunately well-preserved in this case, depicting famous personalities of the Franciscan order, have led to this hall being called the «Sala Morone». When constituted this library was greatly enriched by a splendid donation of volumes by count Lionello

Sagramoso. The fifth chapel, the Chapel of the Cross or the Avanzi Chapel, is entirely lined with a noteworthy collection of canvases. The central wall is dominated by a Crucifixion by Francesco Morone, dated 1498, surrounded by the various elements of a polyptych representing the Passion painted by Paolo Morando, called «il Cavazzola», a pupil of Francesco Morone. Vasari describes these canvases in detail and with great enthusiasm, judging them to be «the finest figures this painter ever made». It should however be noted that the present polyptych is in fact a copy, the original having been transferred to the Civic Museum in the 19th century, and now exhibited in the Castelvecchio Museum. On the left-hand wall hangs the canvas depicting the meeting of Mary with Christ, a work by Francesco Caroto, while the Raising of Lazarus is by Antonio Badile, a pupil of Caroto and later master to Paolo Veronese. The other canvases, with scenes from the Passion: Christ taken prisoner, Christ before Pilate, Christ nailed to the cross, as well as the Resurrection on the archway, are by Nicolò Giolfino, cited by Vasari, and then with his surname altered, only as Paolo Farinati's teacher. Giolfino indeed deserved kinder treatment from the father of Italian art history whose silence, due to a lack of comprehension, marked him too strongly in a negative sense. The next chapel is the most monumental of all, an architectural element standing out from the general exterior outline of the church because of the bulk of its high cylindrical form. This is the Pellegrini Chapel, designed by Sanmicheli. Difficulties and hindrances in its construction, begun before 1529 and still unfinished in 1557, were bemoaned by the architect and Vasari, too, echoes his discontent, noting however that the delay in no way «deformed» the construction. On the altar is a canvas of the Madonna and Child with St. Anne, by Bernardino India, dated 1579. The lunette showing the Eternal Father was painted by Pasquale Ottino.

S. Bernardino, façade.

Castelvecchio, exterior.

10

CASTELVECCHIO

The Castelvecchio was the second, after the palace on Piazza dei Signori, and final residence of the Della Scala (or Scaliger) family; built over a period of some twenty years from 1354 to 1375 by Cangrande and Cansignorio, it was immediately complemented by the construction of a splendid three-arched bridge, conceived and created for the exclusive service and use of the inhabitants of the castle. Its position is one which had already been used to mark the limits of the city, first by the Romans with the Gavi Arch, and later by the Commune, whose city walls met the Adige river at this same point. These walls were now used to divide the construction into two distinct parts: the side towards the inner city was destined for purely military use, for the guard corps, that on the external side was for the «Lords'» residence, that is the «Reggia» of today. The two are divided not only by the city walls but also by a deep ditch, refilled at some unknown date but returned to its original state in 1963. Between the «barracks» and the «reggia» crosses the ramp leading to the bridge, flanked near the threshold of the bridge by the «Mastio» tower. The Scaligers left the castle and Verona in 1387, but the Castelvecchio was already established in its military character. The name Castelvecchio is said to have been applied only after 1395, when the Visconti family built the «new» castles of S. Pietro and S. Felice. The years 1805-1810 are of particular importance to the architectural history of the Castelvecchio, because the French, having demolished the Gavi Arch which was connected to the Clock Tower, destroyed part of the latter as well, bringing back the side nearest the street by several metres and for the same reasons of providing more road space, reduced the width of the ditch by five metres,

where it ran along the Corso in front of the castle. During the same period they built the areas ranged along the river in the large courtyard, thus creating an artillery post directly in line with that part of the city held by the Austrians, on the opposite bank of the river.

It was only after the First World War that conditions were such that the castle was finally released from its function as a military installation and became an exhibition space for the Municipality of Verona's collection of Medieval art. The greatest merit for this fortuitous move is due to Professor A. Avena, the then director of the Civic Museum which was at that stage still housed in the Palazzo Pompei, at the Navi bridge. The work entailed in transforming and adapting the Castelvecchio to this new function as museum lasted from 1923 to 1926, particular care and attention being given to reconstructing the architectural complex according to historically accurate criteria as to its original aspect of «reggia». In the «caserma» or barracks, where faithful reconstruction was less of a problem, the two façades overlooking the courtyard were built with architectural elements from palaces in Verona demolished in 1890-93 during the work of construction of the embankments along the Adige. During the Second World War the Castelvecchio witnessed various sad and momentous historic episodes which resulted in the bombing out of the east wing of the courtyard and of the bridge, blown up with mines. In the summer of 1947 a large exhibition of works reinstated after being hidden away for the duration of the war, marked the reopening of the museum. A decisive step in this reopening was the reconstruction of the bridge, directed by P. Gazzola in 1950-51. In 1956 began a new and radical restructuring of the Castelvecchio to incorporate a museum space conceived along modern lines, allowing the work of art greater expressive powers. Work was first concentrated on

the «reggia», completed in 1958. The remaining section, completed in 1964, involved the reorganisation of the entire complex, with various solutions such as the reopening of the way through the «del Morbio» door of the Commune era, and access being cut through the ramp of the bridge, to allow for a better ordered, more rational visit through the Museum.

CASTELVECCHIO, BRIDGE AND COURTYARD

Cangrande II strengthened his defensive position by building, alongside the castle, a bridge over the Adige river which provided a direct link with the road to Bavaria, whence help could be sought in times of trouble, his daughter Elisabetta having been married to Ludwig of Bavaria, Marquis of Brandenburg. The bridge is composed of three spans, decreasing in width from the right to the left banks of the river. The first, main arch has a chord of 48,70 metres and the other two successively of 29,15 and 24,11 metres. To the outer side, towards the Campagnola, the threshold of the bridge was guarded by a tower, demolished in 1802. The bridge withstood the most torrential floods of the river Adige, but was blown up with dynamite on the afternoon of April 25, 1945. It was faithfully reconstructed in 1950-51, under the direction of Professor P. Gazzola.
The façade opposite the entrance to the courtyard of the Castelvecchio is Gothic, having been reconstructed with

Castelvecchio bridge.

The courtyard of the Castelvecchio with the «Mastio» tower.

Courtyard of the Castelvecchio. Statue of Cangrande set in front of the Porta del Morbio (C. Scarpa).

Some Rooms of the Museum.

elements from the Palazzo dei Camerlenghi, demolished to make way for the Adige embankments in 1890-95. To the right is the area of the castle destroyed by bombing on January 4, 1945. To the left, the point where the 12th century city walls were joined to that of the castle of the 14th century.

Immediately to the left of the entrance, and partly backing onto the surrounding wall opposite the Corso are the remains of the foundations of the small church of S. Martino in Acquaro, dating back to the 8th century, which originally gave the castle its name, which was in fact «of S. Martino in Acquaro». Near the passageway through the Porta del Morbio, the equestrian statue of Cangrande dominates from above. This positioning dates only from the reorganization by C. Scarpa, the statue having originally been on the pediment of his tomb above the gate of S. Maria Antica, but struck down by a violent storm.

Castelvecchio, tomb of SS. Sergius e Bacchus.

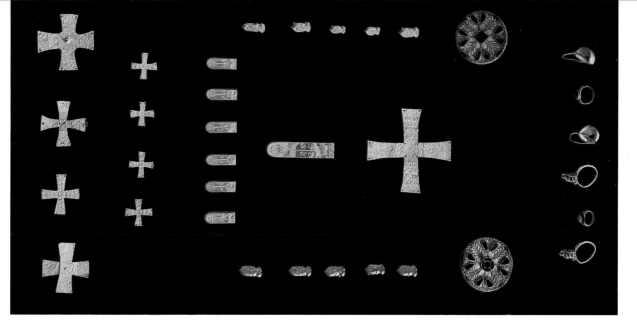

CASTELVECCHIO. SALA TREZZA

Castelvecchio. Barbarian jewellery.

The first room of the **Museum** houses several valuable examples of Romanesque sculpture, ranging from the archivolt by «Magister Peregrinus», to the two «Caryatids» standing back to back, to the cloaked male figure attributed to Brioloto «de Balneo», the sculptor who worked on San Zeno, to the tomb from the church of SS. Sergio e Bacco, which comes from the monastery of S. Silvestro in Nogara, having been taken in the 18th century to the Museo Maffeiano, and hence to the Castelvecchio. The detailed inscription bears the date 1179, that is forty years previous to the porch of San Zeno with which it has been compared, particulary in reference to the Master of the Months. The time difference may be discerned in the greater fluidity of movement in the figures on the tomb.

In a space constructed for the purpose, and projecting beyond the façade of the Museum on the outside, are several works of Barbarian times, such as the small marble urn from S. Giovanni in Valle, of the 6th century, the bronze hand-basin from the Longobard tomb of Via Monte Suello, and the gold ornaments from the same hoard, together with those from Isola Rizza (the so-called Alboin Treasure) and the jewels from a Longobard tomb from Palazzo Maniscalchi.

To the middle of the 14th century belong the two statues in tufa, of St. Bartholomew and St. Cecilia, in the next room, where the Gothic sculpture is housed. St. Cecilia holds a «portativo», portable bellows organ, in her arms.

Most of the sculptures in tufa in this room may be attributed to the «St. Anastasia Master», socalled because his identification is based on the sculpture on the architrave of the main portal of the church of Santa Anastasia. He seems at least partly to coincide with the «Rigino» sculptor, whose work has recently been researched and identified by Mellini, as a powerful expression of a certain line of popular indigenous culture.

A completely different atmosphere informs the small tufa statue of St. Libera (?), previously placed under the projecting archivolt in the church of SS. Siro e Libera at the Teatro Romano. It is 97 centimetres high and has a more subdued character than the larger sculptures. The face is a delicate oval, with the half-closed eyes and the expression of the mouth conferring a sense of pensive withdrawal.

Unfortunately the small tin crown, which so perfectly harmonised with the rich decoration of the garments, was destroyed recently.

THE FOURTH ROOM

The St. Anastasia Master is again represented in the fourth room, with some of his most important works. The group of Marys is part of a Crucifixion with five figures, in the church of Cellore d'Illasi (Verona) where it was taken from its original location in San Fermo, when its very open expression of grief was no longer considered desirable by a citizen requiring its religious images to have more «decorum».

Already in the 14th century a kind of hypocrisy inspired by more refined tastes and customs demanded that the pain of Christ and his mourners should have a more contained expression.

Castelvecchio. Tufa statue of St. James.

Castelvecchio. The Tomba Crucifixion, in tufa.

Under such conditions the somewhat crude dramatic impact of the Crucifixion by the St. Anastasia Master no longer found any place.

The architrave of the portal of this church gives us the exact composition of one of these groups, as does the relief of the «Crucifixion and mourners» in this room of the Museum.

But here the greatest work is the group of Christ Crucified, Mary and St. John, from the church of San Giacomo di Tomba (Verona), which was transferred to the Museum in 1964. It is datable to the second decade of the 14th century, when Cangrande was at the height of his power. The sculptor's strong personality is particulary evident in the figure of Christ, especially in the face with its excruciating expression of grief and pain.

BERNASCONI ROOM

The large room on the first floor overlooking the Adige river is named for Cesare Bernasconi, an eminent art historian and critic, President of the Museum's conservation committee and generous donor of works from his own collection (1871). Here are a large statue of St. John the Baptist from S. Fermo (mid 14th century) and two Crucifixes from the Stations of the Cross. The one from the Assize Courts has two small devotional figures below, and is dated to the mid 14th century; the S. Silvestro work, on a golden ground, has a pelican, as a symbolic image of Christ, in the upper zone, and is of the end of the 14th century.

Castelvecchio. The hall of the «Reggia» overlooking the Adige.

The **panel painting** by Tomaso da Modena showing a kneeling nun between two saints, is useful, despite its unknown origin, as an introduction to Veronese painting in the second half of the 14th century, which doubtless reflected the influence of this painter from Emilia, also active in the Veneto region. Thus alongside this work by Tomaso da Modena we find a detail of the polyptych of the Trinity from the convent of the same name, signed by Turone and dated 1360. Turone was a Veronese painter of Lombard origins, whose connexion with Tomaso da Modena has been demonstrated effectively over the last fifty years.

The painting of the **«Madonna of the Quail»** is attributed with some reserves to the young Pisanello. It was previously in the Galleria Bernasconi. Magagnato maintains that comparison with the Annunciation in S. Fermo provides invaluable evidence in this attribution. Even those who dispute Pisanello's authorship of this work recognise characteristics typical of the great Veronese master, one of the most important figures in Italian art in the second quarter of the 15th century.

Castelvecchio. J. Bellini, St. Jerome in the Desert.

Castelvecchio. Pisanello (?), Madonna of the Quail.

SALA MONGA

The twelfth room, or Sala Monga, contains the panel painting by Jacopo Bellini, **«St. Jerome in the Desert»**, from the Galleria Pompei, a precious example of the work of this great Venetian master. The warm monochrome tones of golden light give the work an almost archaic richness. Jacopo Bellini was in Verona around the year 1436, when he painted a large fresco of the Crucifixion in the Duomo, and at the same time cultivated his interest in the antique, drawing several of the local antiquities.

The painting by Stefano da Verona, called the **«Madonna of the Rosery»**, is from the monastery of S. Domenico in Verona. It represents the theme of the Madonna of Humility in a splendid setting of late Gothic richness, from the painter's mature period, circa 1430. It shows a portion of a celestial field enclosed within the fragile bower of a rose-garden, whose entrance is guarded by a dreaming St. Catherine flanked by peacocks. Angels with the same splendid plumage as the peacocks flutter around the garden, gathering roses, while others sing from the pages of an enormous chorale, others adore the Virgin and Child, and still others decorate a baptismal font with a slender column bearing a polygonal capital rising from its centre.

They are actually not many, but they appear as a shimmering crowd because the flickering dark patches on the golden ground multiply their forms and gestures. In the centre, immersed in somnambulent melancholy, is the Madonna with the Child. It is in these two figures that one most appreciates the obvious links with the art of Michelino da Besozzo, the painter who best represents the Lombard school in International Gothic art.

No better comparison could be made, to illustrate the

confirmed in the fresco of «*St. James led to his martyrdom*» (Ovetari Chapel), where Mantegna painted an archway with an inscription frieze taken from the Arco dei Gavi in Verona. His contact with Verona became more precise when he was commissioned to execute the fine altarpiece at San Zeno which he completed in two years, from 1457 to 1459. It was with the installation of this painting that the art world of Verona was awakened from its late Gothic dream and forced to take account of the reality of changing times. According to Berenson, the Veronese school then developed along two distinct lines. One tendency, led by Domenico Morone,

Castelvecchio. Detail of the statue of St. John the Baptist.

Castelvecchio. A. Mantegna, Holy Family with a female saint.

revolution in Italian art of the first half of the 15th century, than between the work of Stefano and that of Mantegna.

Andrea Mantegna (1431-1506) was born more or less at the time that Stefano painted his «Madonna of the Rosery», a work of timeless beauty, with no precise spatial reference. Mantegna painted the frescoes in the Ovetari Chapel in the church of the Eremitani in 1448-1455, depicting sacred stories specifically set in Imperial Rome within a framework of monumental classical architecture. Mantegna's work here is based on the experience of the influence of Tuscan artists in the Veneto, amongst whom the greatest inspiration was Donatello, although Paolo Uccello and Andrea del Castagno were also of great importance.

Mantegna's revival of the classical was also doubtless encouraged by his father-in-law Jacopo Bellini, whom we have already seen copying antiquities of Verona. His contact with that city must have been early, given the material it offered for study and as an example to be followed in the reconstruction of the antique style. This is

rejected its Medieval heritage and completely embraced the new teachings of Mantegna; the other, headed by Liberale, sought to retain as much as possible of the old repertory. It is Francesco Benaglio, whose «Madonna of the Fan» is shown here, that gives us the first testimony to the enormous impact of the San Zeno altarpiece, from which he drew inspiration, if with somewhat modest results, for his «Triptych of St. Bernardino», dated 1462. The «Madonna of the Fan» once attributed to Morone seems more in keeping with the personality of Benaglio, who creates a monumental perspective setting in Renaissance style, but fails at the same time to people it with sufficiently solid forms. The attribution of the «Madonna and Child with St. Joseph and a Female Saint» to Mantegna's latest phase was reconfirmed, also by Pallucchini, in the occasion of the exhibition of «Masterpieces from the museums of the Veneto» held in Venice in 1946.

Carlo Crivelli, whose «Madonna of the Passion» is exhibited here, was a Venetian painter who in his mature phase moved to live and work in the Marches. The panel in Verona is held to belong to his youthful period and shows how deep was his debt to Mantegna, this influence superseding his early formation on Murano. In the foreground we find a strange confraternity of grotesque figures playing with the instruments of the Passion, represented in a view of a northern landscape on the right.

The proportions of the delicate Madonna are echoed and complemented by a Mantegna-like festoon of fruit.

Less fantastic but of admirable solidity of construction is the work of Saliba, whose «Madonna and Child» is perhaps derived from a lost work by Antonello da Messina, the uncle of the better-known painter of the same name.

SAVERIO DALLA ROSA ROOM

The seventeenth room is named for Saverio Dalla Rosa (1745-1821), a painter and the founder of the civic picture-gallery, created in a time of great social and political transformation. It contains works by Liberale da Verona (circa 1445-1527/8), the painter who viewed the innovations of the San Zeno triptych with a certain detachment, his art developing in many different directions but always retaining strong links with the fantasies of the Gothic. He is particularly noted for his long activity as a miniaturist, the most important example of which is the decoration of the chorales in the Siena Duomo. It has recently been proposed that this activity should be linked with the newly-developing art of graphic printing, basing the theory on his illustration of Aesop's fables for an edition printed in Verona in 1479. His «Madonna and Child with two Angels», or «Madonna of the Goldfinch», like others exhibited here («Deposition from the Cross» and «Nativity with St. Jerome»), show him laying aside his miniaturist's skill («it pleased him greatly to make little things, and he always did so with great diligence, so that they appeared as miniatures» - Vasari) to paint with freedom and vigour, improvising and modifying the painting composition as he worked, and repeating certain details almost as if he had traced them. The front of the wedding-chest, with the «Triumph of Chastity and Love», is a precious illustration of the multifarious activities of a painter's workshop of that time, in which Liberale returns to his taste for «making little things», moving easily and smoothly in the world of allegory.

Castelvecchio. C. Crivelli. Madonna of the Passion.

Castelvecchio. Fr. Benaglio, Madonna of the Fan.

In the **next rooms** we find a good selection of the work of Francesco Bonsignori (circa 1460-1519) a Veronese painter whom Vasari describes as having been influenced by Mantegna from the beginning of his career. Today his formation is seen as more complex, including elements absorbed from both Verona and Venice. Evidently Vasari passed over this less certain phase in the painter's development, to concentrate his biography exclusively on the best-known episode of Bonsignori's life, the period of his sojourn in Mantua as painter to the Gonzaga family, and thus in close contact with Mantegna. Vasari gives 1487 as the date of his move to Mantua. It appears that he was particularly appreciated there as a portrait-painter.

His work in Verona was principally concerned with religious subjects, such as the «Madonna adoring the sleeping Child» his first known work, dated 1483 and signed, which Heinemann defines as Mantegnaesque. The work is dominated by the rigid, metallic folds and corners of the drapery. The nearby «Madonna of the Ox» has evinced suggestions of the influence of the Venetian painter Alvise Vivarini. This room also contains a number of works by Francesco Morone, another Veronese painter who learnt the lesson taught by Mantegna through the severe interpretation of his father Domenico. Francesco Morone shows himself an inspired illustrator of the fervid mysticism which followed the preaching of St. Bernardino. There are also works by several Veneto painters, the most noteworthy being Giovanni Bellini with a Madonna illustrated here, datable to circa 1470. The other work, a Christ Child asleep, is judged to be from his workshop.

Castelvecchio. Fr. Bonsignori, Madonna watching the Child.

THE CAVAZZOLA ROOM

The 23rd room is dominated by the polyptych by Paolo Morando, called Cavazzola, depicting the «Passion of Christ». The work is from the church of San Bernardino, where it has been replaced by a copy. The part illustrated here is the key to the whole composition, dated 1417. Vasari writes of Cavazzola with great admiration, and greatly bemourns his early death in 1522, when he was little more than thirty years of age. «*He was a disciple of Francesco's* (Morone), *and knew much more than his master*». In the large polyptych he demonstrates his ability to construct figures whose marked plasticity does not detract from their vitality, and at the same time shows his mastery as a portrait-painter. Vasari indicates the «young man with a red beard wearing a cap» near the cross as his self-portrait. Of particular value today is the landscape passage showing the Colle di San Pietro before the Venetians built there, between the rocks and the cross. Also represented here is G. Francesco Caroto (circa 1480-1555). He was originally a member of Liberale's workshop but was then attracted to the work of Mantegna «*and thus he went to Mantua and placed himself with him, and learnt so much in so short a time that Andrea sent out a work by his hand, claimimg it his own*» (Vasari). Caroto was a consummately receptive and eclectic artist and during his long and hard-working life passed through various experiences, from his beginnings with Mantegna to his later fascination with great masters such as Leonardo and Raphael. His «Portrait of a young monk» and «Boy with drawing» are illustrated here. In the next room we find his «Pietà with Mary weeping», or «Dead Christ in His mother's arms with St. John».

Castelvecchio. P. Morando (Cavazzola), St. Bernardino polyptych.

STATUE OF CANGRANDE

Facing the early 12th-century wall built by the first Commune of Verona is the equestrian statue of Cangrande, placed here in 1964 when the Museum was restructured. Cangrande, the most famous member of the Della Scala family, was lord of Verona from 1311 to 1329 and a strong supporter of the Imperial cause in Italy. In 1324 he enlarged the city walls, giving Verona a city space which sufficed until the first decades of this century. So the city proper was surrounded by a vast, scarcely occupied space for military operations and better still for the cultivation of vegetables and other necessities, all within the protection of strong enclosing walls. It may thus be understood that Cangrande was exclusively motivated by military considerations, wishing to create a city at once well protected and able to sustain a long seige. This enlargement of the city walls also facilitated the building of the Castelvecchio between the two lines of ramparts.

Castelvecchio. Statue of Cangrande.

The Castelvecchio contains an excellent selection of the work of a great Veronese painter, **Girolamo Dai Libri** (1474-1555). His surmane derives from his family's traditional occupation of illuminating manuscripts, in which Girolamo was judged peerless by his contemporaries. He learnt from his father Francesco, a celebrated miniaturist, and painting also from Francesco Morone, who Vasari says was «a very great friend, almost a brother». Vasari seems to appreciate particularly his sensitive rendering of Nature and narrates in support of this opinion, the tale of the laurel tree that had, from branch to branch, «so clear and comely an air» as to appear «truly a living tree, dainty and most natural»; rather than a praise of naturalism in itself, we are struck by the recognition of the value of the «clear and comely air» in the sacred landscape. The illustration shows his «Nativity with rabbits» of the first years of the 16th century where the painter draws our attention to every last minute detail of reality. Vasari when writing of this work, then in the church of S. Maria in Organo, cites the presence of the rabbits as a qualifying title. Also exhibited is the «Madonna of the Umbrella», signed and dated 1530, in which the painter reveals a reminiscence of Mantegna, and the «Madonna of the oak-tree», certainly of a later date. Here the landscape has a breadth and depth hitherto not seen in his works.

PAOLO CALIARI IL VERONESE

The most famous artist from Verona, Paolo Caliari (1528-1588), called Veronese, is represented in the Museum by a youthful work, the «Bevilacqua altarpiece», from the church

Castelvecchio. Veronese, Deposition from St. Mary of Victory.

of San Fermo, and one from his mature period, the «Deposition», from the church of S. Maria della Vittoria. The first was painted when he was barely twenty, just after he left the workshop of his master, Antonio Badile; the second belongs to the period of his mature, well-known style.

Apart from the canvases which we find catalogued in the Bevilacqua collection at the end of the century, (others were in the Canossa collection), Paolo Veronese had two other works of particular importance in Verona. These were the «Martyrdom of St. George» in the church of the same name, and the «Last Supper». formerly in the monastery of S. Nazaro and now in the «Galleria Sabauda» in Turin. A contemporary of Veronese was Paolo Farinati (1524-1606), who proved a worthy rival in the competition to paint four canvases for the Duomo of Mantua. He was a particularly prolific worker and has left a most valuable «Diary» of his activities. A friend of Veronese, (he was also a witness at his wedding), he did not follow his example in settling elsewhere and remained faithful to his native city. Here we may admire his «Christ before the people», signed and dated 1562, in which may be discerned Mannerist characteristics derived from the Emilian school, and from Michelangelo.
The Museum houses a good selection of works by the great Venetian master Jacopo Tintoretto (1518-1594), also present in Verona in the church of S. Giorgio with a «Baptism of Christ». Here several of his youthful works are exhibited, the «Concert», once the cover of a spinnet, «Four Biblical Stories», once the back of a cupboard; from his mature period are the «Madonna nursing the Child» and the «Adoration of the Shepherds».

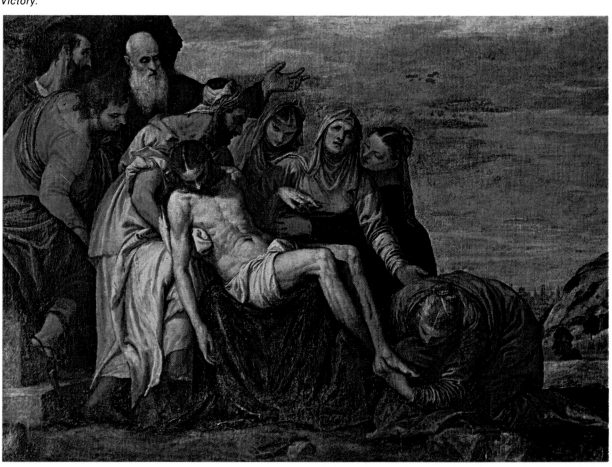

The first «Caravaggesque» painter in Verona seems to have been Pietro Bernardi, who died in 1623. His works are few, undoubtedly because of his early death, but the Museum offers a representative example in the «Holy Family with St. Anne and St. Joachim», with its few figures of a popular character emerging from the dark shadows of a carpenter's workshop. The most profound interpretation of Caravaggio's spirit in Verona, was, however, that of Marcantonio Bassetti (1586-1630), well represented in the Museum. The works range from a copy of Caravaggio's «The Incredulity of St. Thomas» to several portraits of austere seriousness: «Old Nun», «Old man with gloves» (illustrated here), «Old man reading». The cultural comparisons at times brought to mind (as well as Caravaggio, Fetti and Strozzi) all point to a reconsideration of Caravaggio's message.

Besides Bassetti there are two other artists of prime importance in Verona at the beginning of the seventeenth century, Pasquale Ottino and Alessandro Turchi, both pupils of Felice Brusasorzi, as was Bassetti himself. Around 1620 the three painters collaborated on the decoration of the Chapel of the Innocents in the church of S. Stefano, each contributing one canvas. Bassetti and Ottino fell victims to the plague of 1630, while Turchi moved to Rome and worked there until his death in 1649. Amongst the works exhibited is Pasquale Ottino's «Deposition from the Cross» with the portrait of the donor, Count Agostino Giusti. Like others of his contemporaries Ottino experimented on «paragon» stone panels which provided a naturally dark ground, an ideal base in a period when shadow and deep shades were essential to the composition. Amongst the «paragons» exhibited is Ottino's «Temptation of Joseph». Alessandro Turchi, who maintained contact with his native city after his move to the capital, soon developed more classicizing tendencies thanks to the influence of the Bolognese school. The «Flagellation of Christ» is his.

Of uncertain authorship, though long attributed to Paolo Veronese, is the large canvas with the portrait of Pase Guarienti in the military garb of «cataphractorum equitum gubernator», leader of heavy-armed cavalry. It is most unfortunate that such a work, dated with precision to 1556, and coming from an illustrious and ancient Veronese family, should still be of doubtful attribution.
With the end of the panorama of 16th century painting, the successive rooms are dedicated to the crisis in the arts which followed on the heels of the certainties of the Renaissance. The revolution began in Rome with the work of Michelangelo Merisi, called Caravaggio. Artists in Verona were not insensitive to this call for a more severe morality in life and in religious expression, and the great themes of Christian piety found new forms, closer to human reality.

Castelvecchio. D. Brusasorzi (?), portrait of Pase Guarienti.

Castelvecchio. M. Bassetti, portrait of an old man with a glove.

23

Castelvecchio. G.B. Tiepolo, design for a ceiling.

After about 1630, when plague ravaged the city, art in Verona is traditionally considered to have suffered a decline, a period of obscurity which lasted until the early years of the following century, when **Antonio Balestra** (1666-1740) achieved something of a revival. Balestra received his training as an artist in Venice and Rome, and was a prolific worker, his style a delicate balance between Classicist vision and Rococo spirit. Of note is his **self-portrait.** But the last room of the Museum, named for Antonio Avena and dedicated to 18th century painting, concentrates rather on painters who are entirely at home in their time, beginning with **G.B. Tiepolo** and his «Design for the ceiling of Ca' Rezzonico» in Venice (1758). With a small painting by Pietro Longhi entitled «Venetian Family» we find ourselves plunged into the painter's most characteristic world, observed and illustrated with such veiled irony, such absense of condemnation; the decadence of a world entirely centred upon the repetition of immutable domestic ritual. Two small canvases by Francesco Guardi, «Seascape with Ruins» and «Fantastic Landscape» provide characteristic interpretations of the theme of the Venetian landscape, seen not as an objective reality but rather through a vision of fantasy, a distinct foretaste of Romanticism.

A completely different atmosphere is generated by the painting of Luca Giordano, well represented here with three works, «Allegory of Summer», «Diana and Endymion» and «Bacchus and Ariadne». The great Neapolitan painter, consummate master of the most intrepid Baroque virtuosity,

enriched by his Venetian experiences to produce a joyous sensuality of colour and form, already heralds the 18th century, particularly in the two mythological works. In the same room is a work to which recent restoration has restored its correct attribution: the «Adoration of the Shepherds», formerly in the Bernasconi collection, was believed to be by the Emilian painter Bartolomeo Schedoni. Documentary evidence of its coming from Venice and closer stylistic analysis made possible by the restoration, have resulted in its attribution (S. Marinelli) to the Venetian Federico Bencovich (1667-1753), friend and contemporary of Piazzetta and like him, though to a different degree, an element in Tiepolo's formation. The first place in 18th century Veronese painting is held by Giambettino Cignaroli (1706-1770), who also enjoyed wide acclaim outside his city. His special merit as regards Verona is his having obtained official recognition from the Venetian Republic for the local «Academy of Painting», still operating today, which was very justly named after him. His «Transfiguration of Christ» is exhibited here, a tense and moving documentation of a dramatic subject where the influence of Piazzetta may be clearly seen.

24

Piazzetta Castelvecchio, Arco dei Gavi.

THE ARCO DEI GAVI

The Arco dei Gavi is a Roman triumphal monument which until 1805 backed onto the Clock Tower of Castelvecchio.

Demolished by the French to allow for greater traffic mobility, it was reconstructed in 1932 in the present small square.

It was originally built on the edge of a preconstituted area of enlargement of the Roman city, which found its natural limits here because of a breach in the river bank.

The gens Gavia, one of the foremost families in the city in Roman times, were honoured by the Council **(ordo decurionum)** with an arch on public ground for some act of public benefit. They were certainly content with the honour, and constructed the arch at their own expense, around the middle of the first century A.D. The arch offers a particularly rare and precious detail, the signature of the architect, repeated twice. His name was **L(ucius) Vitruvius L(uci) l(ibertus) Cerdo.** It has been suggested that this may be interpreted as indicating a freeman of the famous Vitruvius, the architectural theoretician of the Augustan age. The arch, unlike the gates of Roman Verona, is composed of a single barrel vault, but with openings in the short sides which lend a sense of space in four directions, like the arches over crossroads.

The interior has a horizontal coffered ceiling. The two principal sides have a niche in each of the two piers, from which we may deduce that they were ornamented with four statues of members of the gens Gavia honoured by the arch. The names of two of them are engraved under their respective niches.

Corso Cavour, Palazzo Canossa.

PALAZZO CANOSSA

Palazzo Canossa is perhaps the most illustrious example of civic architecture built by Michele Sanmicheli in Verona, and is the only one still inhabited by the family for which it was originally built. The Canossas moved there in about 1535 when only the central part was completed. The two wings facing the Adige river and forming the courtyard were built in the second half of the 17th century, presumably after Sanmicheli's original design. The external balustrade decorated with marble statues by Giuseppe Antonio Schiavi is of the second half of the 18th century and was presumably built to conceal a raising of the roof. The ceiling of the central hall with its frescoes by Ticpolo (1761) collapsed during the last war, as a result of those same bombardments which struck the nearby wing of the Castelvecchio. Palazzo Canossa has housed important art collections, like that created in the second half of the 16th century by Count Girolamo Canossa, who died in 1591. His collection was sold to Duke Vincenzo Gonzaga of Mantua in 1604, and a more modest collection was again created during the 18th century.

PALAZZO BEVILACQUA

Palazzo Bevilacqua, another solemn work by Sanmicheli, is considered to be more or less contemporary with Palazzo Canossa, and yet presents certain fundamental differences. The more vehement «Roman-ness» of Palazzo Bevilacqua is probably due to its proximity to the Roman Porta dei Borsari, from which Sanmicheli borrowed the motif of the twisted columns and the smaller door frames, with triangular and curvilinear tympana, just as in the first alignment of windows in the Roman gate. The palace was built for the brothers Antonio and Gregorio Bevilacqua and remained incomplete on the side overlooking Piazza S. Apostoli. Gregorio's son Mario Bevilacqua (1536-1593) enriched it with a splendid archeological and art collection which remained substantially intact until the beginning of the 19th century.

Corso Cavour, Palazzo Bevilacqua.

S. LORENZO AND PORTA PALIO

Opposite Palazzo Bevilacqua, which is now a school, a gate leads into a small courtyard beside the Romanesque church of S. Lorenzo. From the façade emerge two robust cylindrical towers of alternating bands of tufa and brick, by which one gained access to the «matronei». These women's galleries dominate the interior of the church, running above the two lateral naves and joined by a section in front, above the narthex. The cruciform plan includes three apses at the ends of the naves and two in the transept, facing in the same direction as the others.

Around the middle of the 16th century Sanmicheli built the monumental Porta Palio, which concludes and epitomises the classical rhythm of the stately road stretching from S. Anastasia to Porta Borsari, to the Arco dei Gavi and hence the Porta Palio, flanked by the façade of Palazzo Bevilacqua, which was designed double its width, and Palazzo Canossa. The external façade of the Porta Palio, with its three apertures surmounted by the busts of mythical warriors, seems to be a backdrop for a Greek trilogy. The internal façade has five large arches.

Porta Palio.

Corso Cavour, church of S. Lorenzo, interior.

Porta Borsari.

The best-conserved of the Roman gates in Verona, the **Porta dei Borsari,** was so named in Medieval times for those who exacted the toll duty **(Bursarii)** on goods in transit. The entire façade facing the countryside has remained intact. Long ago historians of Verona recognised the inscription engraved on the entablature, which records Gallienus' work of reconstruction of the city walls between April and December of the year 265, as later than the gate itself and as having been engraved over the top of an earlier inscription which was thus lost. The **Porta dei Borsari** was most probably built immediately before the Porta Leoni, during the reign of the emperor Claudius (41-54 A.D.), as may be ascertained from its similarity to the now destroyed **Porta Aurea** in Ravenna, which bore the exact date of 43 A.D. The gate is composed of three superimposed orders and rises complete from the ground, the original Roman level having been excavated in 1813. The two barrel vaults on ground level (3,55 metres wide and 4,12 high) are framed by fluted half-columns with Corinthian capitals which support the entablature and the pediment; above is a first series of six windows, behind which there was originally a gallery, and then a further series of the same number, the entire complex rising to a height of thirteen metres and built of white Veronese marble. In 1860 roadworks led to the recovery of the entire foundations of the Roman gate, so that we now know that the interior façade was 17,80 metres from that which we see today. Considering these gigantic proportions the present slender curtain of stone may seem of small account, yet one has no sensation of its being the mutilated remains of something far greater, because it was conceived in its own right as an architectural «mise en scène», heralding the monumental nature of the city.

Piazza Bra. The Arena seen from the Liston.

PIAZZA BRA

The Forum Boarium of Medieval Verona later became Piazza Bra, also known as Braida (church of S. Giorgio in Braida) which may be traced etymologically to the German **breit,** wide. The piazza is bounded by the **Arena,** the line of palazzos on the **Liston,** the 17th-century building of the **Gran Guardia,** and the Neoclassical town hall. Sanmicheli and his school also contributed much to the definition of the form of the square, the former with his **Palazzo degli Honorij,** later Guastaverza and now Palazzo Malfatti, which was begun in 1555. The building is characterized by the lower arcade of five robust arches, which seem to echo the arcades of the nearby Amphitheatre. The school of Sanmicheli, whose protagonist here was Domenico Curtoni, drew on this architecture for the plan of the **Gran Guardia,** the large building forming the south side of the Piazza. Partially completed between 1609 and 1614, it was finished in 1821 when the missing part of the upper order was added.

Piazza Bra. The Gran Guardia with the fountain in the foreground.

Verona. "Christmas in the Arena" by the architect Rinaldo Olivieri is the symbol of the recent International Exhibition "Crèches in Art and Tradition".

Performance of Verdi's Rigoletto in the Arena

AMPHITHEATRE

The Amphitheatre was built outside the original city walls of the Republican era, the monumental structure growing up around the elliptical space of the **arena** which measured 74 and 44 metres along its axes. With the added width of the architectural structure the entire complex measures 152 and 122 metres. This structure is formed of four concentric rings, the outermost today retaining only the four archways of the Ala (wing). Originally this external wall was composed of a series of 73 stone pilasters whose sides measured approximately two metres. These pilasters formed 72 archways and supported the two upper orders with the same number of openings, and at the same time communicated with the internal structure of the amphitheatre through barrel vaults, creating an ambulatory 4,40 metres wide. The second ring followed, which today is seen as the exterior of the Arena. It is composed of radial walls delineated on the outer side of the monument by stone pilasters, and joined at their inner extremities into groups by sections of wall following the shape of the ellipse. In several of the spaces thus created are the stairways leading up to second and third levels for the spectators. Beyond the ambulatory is another ring built along the same lines as the preceding and housing the stairways leading up to the first level, followed by another ambulatory and the final ring, a solid wall with the steps leading onto the podium. Each of the three ambulatories has an underground conduit for drainage, and to the same purpose there are two rectilinear drainage lines constructed along the two axes of the ellipse. Another important underground construction is the rectangular cavity, 36 metres by 8 and 2 metres deep, aligned with the long axis in the centre of the arena. The Ala, and hence presumably the original outer wall, is 30,75 metres high, while today the external wall is for the most part 18,40 metres high. Inside, the actual space of the arena is a modern arrangement, the result of restoration work carried out between 1569 and 1680, under the Venetian Republic. The Amphitheatre of Verona must have already been completed by about 30 A.D., judging from mosaics showing three scenes of gladiators fighting in an amphitheatre which came from a Roman house on Via Diaz, near Porta Borsari and are now in the Archeological Museum. Another highly appreciated spectacle was the **venationes,** or wild beast hunt, while the bronze hand of a boxer, covered with the **caestus,** found in the Amphitheatre, gives evidence of another variety of spectacle.

With the advent of Christianity the activities of the Amphitheatre suffered a progressive decline. In 325 the emperor Constantine forbade gladiatorial «performances», although these were actually continued until finally suppressed by the emperor Honorius at the beginning of the 5th century. Theodoric certainly concerned himself with the Amphitheatre, perhaps even carrying out restoration work, and it was from this that the legend of his having built it sprang. During the Middle Ages the Amphitheatre was used for the administration of justice and capital punishment; **trial by combat** and **trials by «God»** were carried out there. The 16th and 17th centuries saw the complex return to more «entertaining» functions, with **fairs** and **tourneys,** and in the 18th century it was given over to bull-baiting and plays, and to an ever-widening panorama of the performing arts, including, after 1856, opera, which has become the characteristic of the Arena in our own times.

◀ *Aerial view of Piazza Bra. To the left is the Town Hall with the hemicycle added to the Neoclassical building after the last war. Beyond the Gran Guardia is the **pronaos** of the Teatro Filarmonico.*

PIAZZA DELLE ERBE

Piazza delle Erbe corresponds with the Forum of the Roman city, whose paving is now 3,50 metres below ground level, as was discovered when the foundations for the flagpole were dug. The Roman forum was wider than the present-day Piazza; the 14th-century **Casa Mazzanti,** one of the few surviving **frescoed houses** of Verona, stands on the alignment of the original Roman buildings delineating the forum, but on the other side the modern buildings have considerably encroached on the open space. Today the only Roman feature of the square is the female statue which Cansignorio used to form the beautiful fountain in the centre of the Piazza in 1368. Mellini suggests that the work of adapting the statue to this end was executed by the sculptor Giovanni di Rigino. The sculpture, popularly known as the «Madonna Verona», was placed atop a large marble basin from the Roman baths, and the head and arms restored. In its hands is a scroll engraved with the motto of the first Commune: **Est iusti latrix urbs haec et laudis amatrix.** Verona is thus a city proud of her justice and desirous of praise, evidently for her beauty. The seal was replaced by one showing the figure of S. Zeno in 1477, but the original motto remained in the hands of the statue which has become the symbol and personification of Verona. Of old the statue was held to be the same one which Valerius Palladius had taken from the Capitol to the Forum in 379 A.D., as one of the oldest Roman inscriptions in Verona recounts. The Capitol, temple of the Capitoline triad of Jupiter, Juno and Minerva, stood on one of the long sides of the Forum where its remains were found in 1914 beneath the buildings on the nearby Piazzetta Tirabosco, with the older and more significant name of **S. Marco «ad carceres».** Possibly the underground remains of the Capitol had become prison cells or dungeons in the popular imagination. Despite the work carried out by the Superintendency of Antiquities in 1957-60, these remains are still not open to the public. They consist of three large intercommunicating chambers, 7,20 metres by 4, surrounded on three sides by a corridor.

Piazza delle Erbe or Market.

Piazza delle Erbe. The Pillory and the Fountain of Madonna Verona.

Piazza delle Erbe. The Fountain of Madonna Verona.

PALAZZO, TORRE DEL COMUNE

Piazza delle Erbe today has a typical medieval «spindle» plan. which Pinali in the last century believed could be traced to the Roman plan and in particular determined by the requirements of gladiatorial spectacles, but in fact the original Forum space with its rigid rectangular organisation was reduced in later times. The Roman forum was succeeded by the **Platea Major** or **Great Square,** «Piazza Maggiore», which name it retained until the end of the 16th century when Maffei named it Piazza Grande. The buildings surrounding it are of various eras, to which modifications have been made to varying degrees over the centuries. Thus the Romanesque **Palazzo del Comune,** the first to the right if one enters the Piazza from Via Cappello, has an 18th-century Neoclassical side facing the Piazza itself. From it rises the **Torre del Comune,** better known in Verona as the Torre dei Lamberti, which since the summer of 1972 has been open to visitors thanks to the installation of a lift. The octagonal belfry, built in 1462-4, is eighty metres above ground and offers a magnificent panorama of the entire city and the surrounding countryside.

Here too one finds the most beautiful and monumental of the bells of Verona, the «Rengo» (from Arringo, literally «Harangue»), cast in 1557 by Alessandro Bonaventurini, member of an illustrious family of Veronese metal-casters whose activity was begun in the second quarter of the century by Don Bonaventura, head priest of Pescantina and Alessandro's uncle. Alessandro continued the family business together with his brother don Gio. Battista and was succeeded by his sons Giulio and Lodovico who continued working until the second decade of the 17th century.

Old Market. The Scala della Ragione.

ARCO DELLA COSTA

In the lower belfry hangs the «Marangona» bell which some hold to have signalled the beginning and end of the craftsmen's working day (marangon means carpenter in the Veronese dialect).

Next to the Palazzo is the **Arco della Costa,** so-called because of the cetacean rib (costa) hung there. Authoritative sources suggest that the arch repeats an ancient plan, described in the rhythmic description of Verona at the time of Pippin, where it mentions four separate arches on the four sides of the Forum. Beyond the Arco della Costa stands the arcaded front of **Casa Mazzanti,** frescoed by the Mantuan painter Alberto Cavalli, a pupil of Giulio Romano, which offers one of the few remaining examples of the custom of frescoing the houses, which led in the past to Verona's being known as a «painted» city.

THE COLUMN OF SAN MARCO

The marble baldachin in the centre of the Piazza was used in the ceremonies of investiture of the **Podestà** and the main public offices. Its steps and pillars are marked with Veronese commercial measures. Near the north end of the Piazza is the **column of S. Marco,** erected in 1523 as testimony to the city's loyalty to the Venetian Republic. Its architect was Michele Leoni, who later worked on the construction of fortifications for the Republic and then was dismissed to make way for Sanmicheli in 1531, to be recalled in 1540. The column stands before the Baroque **Palazzo Maffei,** built as far as the cornice above the piano nobile for Marcantonio Maffei between 1626 and 1630 by an unknown architect, probably from Rome. The present form of the palazzo, with the added row of square windows and the balustrade bearing statues of divinities, was ordered by

Rolandino Maffei, grandson of Marcantonio, and completed in 1668. The palazzo is praised by Scipione Maffei for its having «*the best of four workshops, without spoiling its taste*», and the internal spiral staircase for being «*spacious and noble and all open to the air*», and finally for its hanging garden. Besides the palazzo at the beginning of Corso Porta Borsari rises the **Gardello Tower,** previously known as the **Torre delle Ore,** which Cansignorio had built in 1370. The monumental bell with the image of San Zeno as a fisherman and the Della Scala family seal cast by Master Jacopo «**sub magnifico domino Cansignorio**», now exhibited in the Castelvecchio Museum, is from this tower. Opposite the tower is the house built for Vincenzo Curione between 1558 and 1560, important in local history because it was during the digging of its foundations that the above-cited inscription about the nearby Capitol was found. The Piazzetta IV Novembre on the other long side of the Piazza contains a monument by E. Girelli commemorating the victims of bombings during an air raid in the First World War. There follows the Gothic **Domus Mercatorum** built in 1301 and lavishly restored in 1878. The buildings continuing to the corner with Via Mazzini are those for which the painter Angelo Dall'Oca Bianca, indefatigable defender of the integral unity of the Piazza, fought so hard when they were threatened by plans for the construction of a bank on the site.

PIAZZA DEI SIGNORI

The great bulk of the ancient Palazzo del Comune has an enclosed internal courtyard called the **Mercato Vecchio**, which has recently been used for summer theatre seasons. As is the obvious from the filled in archways, this originally had an arcade also the side towards Piazza delle Erbe. The wide external stairway supported by four different arches was constructed in the mid 15th century and is called the «Scala della Ragione».

Piazza dei Signori, or **Piazza Dante** as it has been called since the erection of a marble statue of the poet in 1865, is

Scaliger Palazzo with the Bombardiera Door.
Piazza Dante.

bounded on the side nearest Piazza Erbe by the **Domus Nova**, a Baroque construction of the second half of the 17th century, but the most prestigious architectural feature here is the 15th-century **Loggia del Consiglio** which marked the beginning of the Veronese Renaissance. If we dismiss Maffei's hypothesis of a certain Fra'Giocondo, we have no idea of who the architect might have been. Working on the construction were the best stonemasons then in the city, mostly Lombards such as Matteo Mazzola, called Panteo, and Gabriele Frisoni, who later worked whith Biagio Rossetti in Ferrara.

The Veronese Domenico da Lugo also worked here with the Lombards. The opening up of the lower floor with a series of eight arches grouped into two series of four each, lends the building the form and name of a «Loggia», if the ample forms of this colonnade have a Tuscan flavour, the taste for colour in the painted sections and the use the three local coloured marbles, red, white and black are unmistakably from Verona, as is seen in the previous use these materials in the same way, on the church of S. Anastasia. The floral decoration of the pilasters and the two-mullioned windows on the upper floor are well-known Lombard motifs. The building is crowned with five statues representing great men of Verona (or presumed of Verona) in antique times: Vitruvius, Catullus, Pliny the Elder, Macrus and Cornelius Nepos. Sculpted and placed there at the end of the century, their «Roman-ness» is rather lacking in credibility and they appear more as the figures of saints.

Archeological remains.

Arche Scaligere:
the monument to Cansignorio.

THE ARCHE AND S. MARIA ANTICA

Near the small church of S. Maria Antica, amidst the Scaliger palaces which now house the Prefecture and the Tribunal, is the small enclosure of the «Arche», as the cemetery of the Della Scala family is now known. Above the side door of the church is the aedicule or «shrine» containing the sarcophagus of Cangrande, who died in 1329. The spired roof forms a pedestal for the copy of the equestrian statue now in the Castelvecchio Museum. In the «smiling» face of the warrior and the simultaneous movement of his body and of the horse beneath him we find not only vitality and boundless energy, but also a benevolent consideration of those around him. Under the aedicule he is instead composed upon his death bed, but with the same smiling expression which leads to comparison with the **«San Zeno laughing».** Cangrande's tomb is outside the small cemetery, which is enclosed by a wall of Veronese stone with a flexible wrought iron mesh grille above it. Inside this space the oldest sepulchre, dating to 1277, is the sarcophagus of Mastino I, completely devoid of any figurative element. On the other hand, the **sarcophagus of Alberto I,** who died in 1301 (some hold this to be a temporary tomb for Cangrande), has figurative decoration on the long walls and at the sides. On one side we see the nobleman kneeling with the Virgin enthroned with angels, on the other he is on horseback between Mary Magdalene and St. James of Compostella. Much more elaborate is the **monument to Mastino II,** which he himself had built during his lifetime, between 1340 and 1350. The monument has its own quadrangular enclosure and the four pilasters at the corners support female statues, of which two are antique, now undergoing restoration at the Castelvecchio Museum. The entire monument is at present enclosed by brick walls in preparation for its complete restoration. The long wall of the sarcophagus facing the street shows Mastino II presented to God-the-Father by St. George, while there is a Crucifixion on one of the short sides. The tympana crowning the four sides of the aedicule are decorated with four episodes from Genesis: Original Sin, the labours of Adam and Eve, Cain and Abel and the Drunkenness of Noah. At the top of the spire is the equestrian statue of Mastino II, enveloped in anonimity by his armour. The most ambitious funeral monument is that to Cansignorio. He, like his father Mastino II, provided for his eternal rest while still alive, building a mausoleum which however was not, it seems, completely finished at his death in 1375, as shown by his having been temporarily laid to rest in the church of S. Maria Antica. The mausoleum has a hexagonal plan and is signed by **Bonino da Campione.** The enclosing wall has corner pilasters with a warrior saint on each, protected by a cuspidate aedicule. On a level with these saints is the sarcophagus, decorated all around with scenes from the Life of Christ and the presentation of Cansignorio to the Virgin. On the cover lies the figure of the dead man, watched over by four angels. Higher up the motif of the six corner aedicules is repeated, this time with six angels, each holding the coat-of-arms of the Della Scala family. The hexagonal pyramid supporting the equestrian statue becomes a plinth with six faces higher up, with two apostles sculpted on each face. Dominating all is the equestrian statue of Cansignorio, rigid and inert compared with that of Cangrande,

Arche Scaligere: interior of S. Maria Antica.

Via Arche Scaligere: "Romeo's House".

ROMEO'S HOUSE

A few steps from the Arche is an example of civic architecture, part Romanesque and part Gothic, linked by tradition to the most famous story of love and death in literature, Romeo and Juliet. The wall of the courtyard of the house indicated as **«Romeo's House»,** that is the house of the Montecchi or «Montagues», actually overlooks Via Arche Scaligere. History teaches that the Monticoli family, the head of the Ghibelline party, was the first family in Verona until the hostility of the Della Scala family forced its members to abandon the city; they later settled in Udine. Attempts have been made in the past and again recently to redeem the complex, originally far more extensive, but in vain, just as research in the archives to provide some substantiation of the legend have rather tended to negate the whole story.

JULIET'S HOUSE

A tale by Luigi Da Porto of Vicenza, published in Venice in 1531, narrates the vicissitudes of two unhappy lovers in Verona, Romeo Montecchi and Juliet Capuleti. Had this tale not been taken up by Shakespeare, Romeo and Juliet today would be no better known than Mariotto and Gianozza, the two unhappy lovers in Siena whose story, no less heartrending than those of the famous lovers, was narrated by Masuccio from Salerno in his «Novellino». Poetry has conferred an authenticity greater than any historical evidence could muster. In fact historical documentation is completely lacking, and this not for want of searching. The most certain fact is that of the rivalry between the families of the Montecchi and the Capuleti, which is also recorded by Dante, an eyewitness to these affairs during his sojourn in the city as guest of Bartolomeo Della Scala, lord of Verona from 1299 to 1304. The Da Porta narrative takes place in these precise years. Juliet is represented as the daughter of Antonio Cappeletti. The name is not however an old Veronese family name; there existed the Dal Cappello family whose house was in fact in the S. Tomio district, perhaps just that same house which tradition indicates as Juliet's. The keystone of the entrance arch to the courtyard does bear a **marble coat-of-arms with a hat** (cappello), which is the noble seal of the family. It cannot however be concluded that Juliet Capulet was from this same Dal Cappello family; on the contrary the name Cappelletti (small hat) would seem to indicate some form of dependence on and inferiority to the other family. Thus the question as to whether this was really the family house of the luckless Juliet remains unsolved. But poetry has the strength to overcome historical pedantry and insists that it was from this balcony that Juliet sealed her tryst with her lover. In the courtyard Juliet's image finds concrete form in the bronze sculpture by the Veronese Nereo Costantini. The interior of the house is in 14th century style, certainly not in its original condition, but recreated faithfully and enriched by a vast selection of Medieval ceramics.

The Statue of Juliet.

Via Cappello: "Juliet's House".

S. Anastasia, façade.

SANT'ANASTASIA

The church of S. Anastasia reveals close similarities with SS. Giovanni e Paolo in Venice. Both churches belonged to the Dominican order and it would be fair to suppose a common architect. The great tripartite brick façade is unfinished. The «Master of S. Anastasia» worked on the portal, sculpting the reliefs on the architrave, at the beginning of the 14th century; the church was consecrated in 1471. The nave is subdivided into aisles by tall cylindrical columns of red Veronese marble joined together by arches, above which the light enters through ample circular windows. The first two columns are flanked by «gobbi», hunchbacked figures, holding the holy water stoups. The older figure, to the left, has been attributed to Gabriele Caliari, the father of Paolo «Veronese». Immediately

following, in the right nave, we find a monument in a mature classicizing style, the **Fregoso Altar,** executed in 1565 by the sculptor Danese Cattaneo. Next, the **Pindemonte Altar,** dedicated to St. Martin, whose traditional image dressed as a knight is the work of the painter G.F. Caroto. The altar built by Francesco the mason in 1535, is an architectural copy of the Arco dei Gavi. In the right arm of the transept is the **Centrego Altar** (1488-1502), with an admirable altarpiece by Girolamo dai Libri, showing the Virgin enthroned between St. Thomas and St. Augustine. In the first chapel of the transept is **Altichiero's** fresco depicting the presentation of various members of the Cavalli family to the Virgin enthroned, datable to circa 1380. The fresco by Pisanello originally on the archivolt leading into the nearby Pellegrini chapel has now been removed to the Sacristy. Painted around 1436, at the height of the Flamboyant Gothic style, it depicts the legend of St. George (see p.62). Inside the **Pellegrini Chapel** itself the fresco by Pisanello recorded by Vasari is no longer visible (it showed St. Eustace caressing a dog), but there are the twenty-four terracottas showing scenes from the Life of Christ (1435-36) of the Florentine school. In the **main Chapel** is the large funeral monument to Cortesia Serego (1432). Returning towards the entrance, we find the **Chapel of the Rosery** (1586-96), immediately after

40

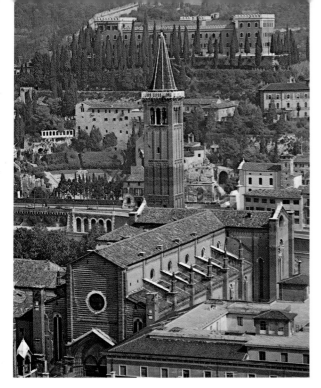

the transept; its name is due to the revival of the practice of telling the rosary following the victory of the Battle of Lepanto. From this we move on to the **Miniscalchi Altar,** also known as the altar of the Holy Spirit, where the architectural relief and the statues have recently been attributed to a certain master Agnolo, a Venetian who was commissioned to execute the work in 1506. He seems to be the same sculptor known to have collaborated with Tullio Lombardo. The altarpiece showing the Holy Spirit descending on the Apostles, was painted in 1518 by Nicola Giolfino, who also painted the altarpiece for the next altar, the **Faella Altar,** depicting the Saviour in Glory with Sts. Erasmus and George below. The architectural structure was executed between 1520 and 1522 by Francesco the mason, already mentioned in connexion with the Pindemonte Altar.

S. Anastasia with S. Pietro hill in the background.

S. Anastasia, Altichiero: The Cavalli family presented to the Virgin.

S. Anastasia, the «Gobbi», the first of them attributed to Veronese's father, G. Caliari.

S. Anastasia, Chapel of the Rosary.

S. Anastasia, Pisanello: St. George and the Princess.

FRESCOES BY PISANELLO AND SOTTORIVA

In the S. Anastasia fresco we see Pisanello as the latest and most melancholy illustrator of those myths that inspired the poetry of the Middle Ages. The knight braving all hardship and peril to defend his lady (Madonna, in the language of the times), is the protagonist of an undertaking across whose multifarious incidents march the most ill-assorted crowds, the most beautiful and most monstrous of animals, the most terrifying landscapes and the most enchanting and enchanted of buildings, the roles of the protagonists in these dramas becoming less and less clearly defined against the shifting panorama. The Gothic marble citadel in the background is perhaps the far-off aspiration and comfort of the crowd of mute wanderers in the desert of horror.

Via Sottoriva, reached from the side of S. Anastasia, offers an image of Medieval Verona, with its arcaded houses that once overlooked the Adige.

Via Sottoriva.

Duomo, façade.

THE DUOMO

The Duomo today is a composite structure of varying styles and epochs, the original Romanesque building having undergone Gothic modifications in the second half of the 15th century. The outer walls in tufa reinforced with great blocks of Veronese stone, particularly on the corners, are entirely as they were in the original structure, while the part most completely conserving its original aspect is in the area of the apse. Near the campanile one may also see the wall of the original «cuba» indicating the height achieved in the 15th century. On the façade the raised part is indicated by bands in the right-hand wall, and at the same time the two large Gothic two-mullioned windows were opened up. The central part with the large porch is more cohesive; the sculptor Nicolò worked here in 1139, after San Zeno. S. Anastasia has an air of greater monumentality compared with San Zeno, and a more moderate use of figurative sculpture. The lunette is decorated with an Annunciation to the Shepherds and the Adoration of the Magi.

THE BELL TOWER

The Campanile with its Romanesque base should have been completed in the 16th century to a design by Sanmicheli but this undertaking failed, according to Vasari, because of the incompetence of those commissioned for its execution. It was finally built in this century after a plan by E. Fagiuoli.

DUOMO. THE INTERIOR

If the exterior of the Duomo has conserved a clearly Romanesque flavour, the interior is entirely Gothic, although the long progress of the minor naves was interrupted by a series of chapels between the end of the 15th and the beginning of the 16th century. In the second chapel to the right is the **Adoration of the Magi** by Liberale, carefully described by Vasari who observes that the minute attention to detail makes it seem a miniature. This and the successive chapel are framed in grandiose architectural forms painted by Falconetto, who gave them the form of Roman triumphal arches seen in perspective. Along this nave is now hung the great **Cross**, formerly in S. Elena, a Venetian work of the early 15th century. There follows the Chapel of the Sacrament where the great fresco of the Crucifixion painted by Jacopo Bellini in about 1436, later destroyed, once hung. At the end of this nave is the **Altar of St. Agatha,** combining a Gothic arch with Renaissance cornices and frames, sculpted in 1508 by the mason Domenico da Lugo.

The area of the presbytery is enclosed by a **choir screen** in the Ionic order, perhaps by Sanmicheli. The frescoes of the apse are by Francesco Torbido, after drawings by Giulio Romano. Returning along the other nave, we immediately find the door leading into the interesting **archeological area** (see p. 60), and at the end of the nave the Cappella Nichesola with Titian's **Assumption,** datable to the years 1535-40. There follows the funeral monument to Galesio Nichesola, attributed to Jacopo Sansovino.

Duomo, porch.

Duomo, interior.   *Duomo. Titian: Assumption of the Virgin*

SANTA MARIA MATRICOLARE

These remains, whose original level has only recently been brought to light, were long held to be the foundations of the church of S. Maria Matricolare, founded in 774 by Bishop Lotherius. Others saw here the Duomo built by Ratherius, bishop from 932 to 968. Arslan however recognised it as contemporary with the Romanesque Duomo, being part of the crypt. Recent works have revealed its connexion with what remains of the plan of the two most ancient Christian basilicas in Verona, in the interior of S. Elena. The larger of these was recognised in the last century, while the other was revealed only recently during excavation inside the church of S. Elena. Arslan has identified the first as Lotherius' S. Maria Matricolare (8th century). The most important feature of the remains are the mosaic floors, which have recently been dated to approximately the end of the 4th century. The smaller basilica seems to be a pagan temple adapted for Christian use, and could thus be dated to the times of Constantine. The larger basilica extends beneath the cloister of the Canons and thence beneath the Biblioteca Capitolare, famous for its collection of ancient codexes.

S. Giovanni in Fonte. One side of the octagonal baptismal font.

SAN GIOVANNI IN FONTE

Behind the Duomo is the small church of **S. Giovanni in Fonte** (12th century) whose apses, with their original beauty unspoiled, may be seen from the courtyard of the bishop's residence. Inside the church is one of the most important examples of Romanesque sculpture in Verona, the **octagonal baptismal font** in red S. Ambrogio stone, its eight sides adorned with scenes from the Life of Christ. It is the work of two sculptors active at the beginning of the 13th century. The one who executed six of the reliefs reveals close affinities with Brioloto, who scupted the «wheel» on the façade of San Zeno.

S. Giovanni in Fonte, interior with the baptismal font in the centre.

Sunset along the Adige.

SAN GIORGIO

The architect of the church is unknown. The design of the cupola and the unfinished campanile are attributed to Sanmicheli and the church is presumed to have been built between 1536 and 1543. The façade was constructed in two stages, the upper zone belonging in fact to the 17th century. The interior is a large hall with four chapels on each side and a wide transept. Above the entrance door is a large canvas by **Tintoretto** showing a «Baptism of Christ». All the altars are decorated with works of high artistic quality, those to the left being perhaps of greater interest, from the St. Ursula and her companions painted by G. F. Caroto in 1545 on the first altar, to his Sts. Rocco and Sebastian on the third, to the «Madonna of the belt with Sts. Zeno and Lawrence» by Girolamo dai Libri, signed and dated 1526. On the third altar to the right is the «Pentecost» by Domenico Tintoretto, and on the fourth the «Madonna in Glory» with angels below, by Felice Brusasorzi. In the transept two Ionic order altars support the organ and the choir. An Ionic balustrade surrounds the presbytery, with six bronze statues cast in Venice in 1625. To the right hangs a large canvas by Paolo Farinati, the **«Miracle of the loaves»,** with Felice Brusasorzi's **«Manna in the desert»,** completed after his death by his pupils, opposite. The end wall of the apse is dominated by the most outstanding work of art in the church, rich as it is in valuable pieces: the **Martyrdom of St. George** by **Paolo Veronese,** painted in 1565-66 during a period of particular creative genius, when the painter returned to Verona to marry Elena Badile, the daughter of his painting master.

S. Giorgio in Braida, on the left side of the Adige.

SANTO STEFANO

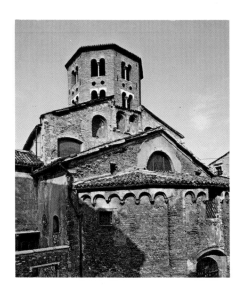

The church of S. Stefano is recorded as having existed in the time of Theodoric. It was built on the left - hand side of the Adige, near the Roman Theatre, on a site previously dedicated to the sanctuary of the Alexandrian divinities Isis and Serapis. Its style is predominantly Romanesque, the most complex monument of this epoch in Verona. Its unique elements are the two ambulatories, one above the other, inside the apse, with capitals taken from earlier monuments, and the octagonal brick tambour with two orders of two-mullioned windows. The church is divided into three naves by simple square pilasters and the transept is considerably raised because of the crypt below. To the right is the Baroque **Chapel of the Innocents** with three important early 17th century canvases, the **Five Bishops** by Marcantonio Bassetti, the **Massacre of the Innocents** by Pasquale Ottino, and the **Forty Martyrs** by Alessandro Turchi.

Of particular note is the 14th-century sculpture of St. Peter seated, from the demolished church of S. Pietro di Castello. To the left of the main altar are two frescoes, the **Annunciation** and the **Coronation of the Virgin,** identified as works of the central period of Martino da Verona, a noted painter of the times of Altichiero who died towards the end of 1412.

ROMAN THEATRE

The Roman Theatre as we see it today is the result of a series of archeological interventions carried out for the most part between 1834 and 1914. Until 1844 these excavations were undertaken by Andrea Monga, who had bought the land precisely for this purpose, at considerable expense and with somewhat modest results in a visual sense, revealing the hollow spaces for the most part, but

The apse of S. Stefano with the drum above.

The city seen from the Colle S. Pietro. In the foreground is the Teatro Romano, with the Ponte Pietra beyond.

The Teatro Romano. To the right is the small church of SS. Siro e Libera. Above the cavea stands the former monastery of. S. Girolamo, now the Archeological Museum.

arriving at a good overall knowledge of the monument, which information was subsequently reworked and published by Serafino Ricci in 1895 with the hope that Monga's example would inspire the authorities to continue his work. In 1904 Monga's heirs sold the property to the Municipality of Verona, and the work of demolition and excavation to reveal what remained of the ancient monument began under the direction of Prof. G. Ghirardini from the faculty of Archeology at the University of Padua. It was wisely decided to leave untouched the small church of SS. Siro e Libera whose demolition would have contributed nothing to furthering our knowledge of the monument itself, and which at the same time offers precious information regarding its decline and trasformation. The Roman Theatre backs onto the slope of Colle di S. Pietro. The orchestra has a diameter of 100 feet (29,64 metres). The cavea was divided into at least two sections, the **ima** and the **summa cavea,** crowned by two galleries, and altogether reached a height of 27 metres, as is indicated with reasonable accuracy by the series of ten small archways in Veronese stone, known as the «loggette», connected to the ancient monastery building to the west in 1912. The Theatre has been dated to the last quarter of the Ist century B.C.

Archeological Museum, a hall.

Archeological Museum. Bronze head from the Augustan period.

ARCHEOLOGICAL MUSEUM

The building which stands over the cavea is the former **Monastery of the Gesuati** or of **S. Girolamo,** begun in 1429. In 1508 the painter G.F. Caroto completed and signed the Annunciation in the small monastery church. The order of Friars Preachers (Gesuati), was suppressed in 1668 so that Venice could continue the War of Candia with the proceeds from the sale of their property. The monastery was acquired by the Friars Minor Conventual in 1671 and the brothers of that order occupied it until suppressed in 1769. It then became private property and the «Camilione Monga», later the property of the City of Verona, and an Archeological Museum in 1923. The museum section was restructured in 1956-59, and the complex still awaits completion. Of particular note, in the entrance hall, is the statue of **Imperator** from vicolo S. Clemente, and the portrait of Gaius Caesar, Augustus' nephew, who died in 4 A.D., from Piazza Duomo, as well as the mosaic showing gladiators from Via Diaz and those from Villa Negrar in Verona. Amongst the small Roman bronzes (2nd room) we mention particularly those found locally: the Priapus of Montorio, the Lar of Tregnago, the Combattants from Isola della Scala, the Isis Fate from the Adige, and the man wearing a toga from the Duomo. In the 3rd room, beside the glassware from the hoard of a Veronese tomb, the bronze head from Pestrino, a powerful portrait of a personage of the Augustan age, is of particular note. Pestrino is on the southern edge of Verona, near the Adige. In the Refectory the most important work is a copy of a seated Aphrodite of the times of Phidias and a large standing female statue, perhaps a cult statue, both from Piazza del Duomo. Next in importance to these is the Orator donated by Pinali, previously in a private Venetian collection, similar in arrangement to the Lateran Sophocles. In the small church of S. Girolamo are the small statue of the Good Shepherd, datable to the 4th century, previously in the Museo Maffeiano, and two wooden models, one of the Arena (mid 18th century) and the other of the Arco dei Gavi (early 19th century).

Roman Theatre and Archeological Museum. Head of Dionysus from the Theatre

The Ponte Pietra and the Colle di S. Pietro.

S. Giovanni in Valle.

PONTE PIETRA

The work of reconstructing the bridge blown up in April 1945 was begun in February 1957, using as far as possible the original material salvaged from the bed of the Adige and classified with much patient research. The bridge had already suffered wide damage and subsequent repairs in previous centuries, so that in 1945 the only Roman arches were the first two from the left, while the others were from the times of the Della Scala family (first to the right) and from the 16th century (those in brick). The dentils at road level on the exterior are believed to be supports for a Medieval acqueduct. In Roman times the Ponte della Pietra (literally, stone bridge) and further downstream, once on a level with the apse of S. Anastasia, the now-destroyed **Ponte Postumio,** formed a frame for the Roman Theatre and the monumental complex on the slope of Colle di S. Pietro overlooking the city.

CHURCH OF SAN GIOVANNI IN VALLE

The small valley to the east of Colle di S. Pietro gives us the name of a small church, already recorded in the 8th century: **S. Giovanni in Valle.** The present church has a 12th-century plan and is typical of Veronese Romanesque architecture. Two sarcophagi in the crypt confirm this as the site of an earlier cemetery, ot the beginning of the Christian era, similar to the examples in S. Stefano and S. Elena. Restoration work carried out on the façade after the last war has reinstated the original small windows of Romanesque outline which had been replaced by large windows with mouldings in the 17th century. More characteristic and complete is the area of the apse, whose beauty is comparable to that of S. Giovanni in Fonte. On the right-hand side there remains standing one side of the cloister and part of the Romanesque campanile, with its 16th century belfry.

SANTA MARIA IN ORGANO

In 1481 monks of the Olivetan order began the renovation of the ancient church of S. Maria in Organo. The campanile designed by Fra' Giovanni da Verona was completed in 1535, and in 1547 Michele Sanmicheli entrusted the execution of his plan for the façade to his cousin Paolo, the work however remaining unfinished.

THE INTERIOR

The interior is divided into three naves, with a row of chapels on each side. The area designated for the congregation is developed in four bays, at the end of which a series of steps leads up to the raised section, which comprises the

S. Giovanni in Valle, remains of the cloisters and the campanile.

S. Maria in Organo.

S. Maria in Organo, interior.

S. Maria in Organo, marquetry by Fra' Giovanni da Verona.

presbytery, transept and annexes. The elevation of this section is due to the presence of the crypt, whose entrance was closed in 1600 with the construction of the steps. Above the central nave N. Giolfino (to the left) and G.F. Caroto (to the right) executed frescoes with scenes from the Old Testament. In the third chapel to the left is the «Madonna enthroned between Sts. Martin and Augustine» signed and dated in 1503 by Francesco Morone. Francesco's father Domenico frescoed the cupola with twelve angels playing musical instruments between 1497 and 1499. His too are the busts of the four evangelists with their relative symbols and the four doctors of the church on the ceiling of the transept. In the presbytery are the large canvases by Paolo Farinati, but what catches the attention here is the marquetry on the backs of the choir stalls executed by Fra' Giovanni da Verona around the year 1499. Fra' Giovanni worked again in S. Maria in Organo after 1519, when he executed the marquetry of the cupboards in the sacristy. Here the portraits of the Olivetan fathers frescoed above the cupboards are the work of Francesco Morone, while the landscapes were painted on the cupboards by Agostino and Domenico Brusasorzi, the six landscapes in the presbytery being signed by G.F. Caroto.

PALAZZO GIUSTI AND THE GIUSTI GARDEN

Palazzo Giusti del Giardino was laid out in its present form in the last decade of the 16th century by Count Agostino Giusti who completed the work by commissioning Orazio Farinati to fresco the façade with allegorical figures of Faith, Hope, Charity and Justice in 1591. According to Pona the palazzo was built «for the purpose of literary conversation». In fact it is known that Count Agostino Giusti, member of a philharmonic academy, gathered **a literary circle** around him in his house. He is also remembered as a collector of artworks and antiquities, engaging in something of a competition with his son-in-law Mario Bevilacqua. Unfortunately his collection, augmented by his son Gio.Giacomo, was dispersed as early as 1641, although the ancient inscriptions laid out in the gardens survived, so that in 1648 Lisca and Cozza were able to list twenty-eight Latin epigraphs, most of them still extant, with the addition of other antiquities from the collection of the Venetian Molin. The garden was further embellished with fountains, a fishpond, a **labyrinth** and a **citrus grove** adorned with statues, and also an aviary, **«the place where a variety of flying creatures are conserved».** Despite the inevitable damage and alterations which the garden has undergone, it still retains its fascination for the poetic contests of those nobles who frequented the literary circle of Agostino Giusti. In our own times the garden has on occasion provided an exceptional backdrop to events from the Summer Theatre of Verona.

Palazzo Pompei, Civic Natural Science Museum.

Giusti Garden.

S. FERMO

Two superimposed churches combine to make S. Fermo the uniquely beautiful and important complex it is today. The lower church retains unchanged its original Romanesque plan, while the upper church was radically altered by the Franciscans who succeeded the Benedictine monks in 1261, creating here its predominantly Gothic aspect. The Franciscans began their work of renovation in the first decades of the 14th century and completed it only in the final years of that century. Successive centuries saw this church, as so many others, disfigured by indiscriminate additions and modifications, until the beginning of this century when an extensive programme of restoration brought it to its present condition. Much of the work was concerned with freeing the apses from the miserable secondary structures enclosing and effectively hiding them. It is precisely this part of the church around the apses that permits us to ascertain that the Gothic church was built over the Romanesque edifice already standing; the main apse is in fact Romanesque in the lower section, abruptly cut off where the body of the Gothic apse begins. The three minor apses are also Romanesque, although partially rebuilt, as is the campanile.

PALAZZO POMPEI. SCIENCE MUSEUM

Palazzo Pompei on the left bank of the Adige near Ponte Navi, has been traditionally attributed to Sanmicheli since Vasari's times. It was Olimpia Lavezzola's dowry when she married Alessandro Pompei in 1579. In 1852 the palace was bequeathed to the city of Verona and the Civic Museum was inaugurated there in 1857. The art and archeological collections were later transferred elsewhere and since 1926 Palazzo Pompei has been the seat of the Natural Science Museum. The present layout of the Museum was established after work finished in 1965, with nineteen rooms on two floors. Particular mention should be made of the two rooms on the ground floor immediately to the right of the entrance, which contain general and Veronese prehistorical exhibits, and after the atrium housing temporary exhibitions and the covered courtyard, fhe room containing the **fossils from Bolca** (Vestenanuova, Verona) with its extensive collection of thirty-eight cases of fossils, ranging from fish to palms, to reptiles and tortoises. Part of the collection comes from the rich deposits at Avesa, a few kilometres west of the city. Continuing on through the Museum one finds a fine variety of exhibits including minerals, rocks, invertebrates, insects, Italian and exotic birds, amphibians and reptiles.

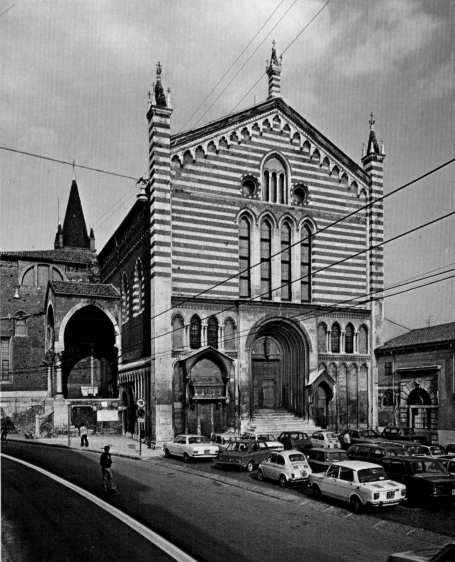

S. Fermo Maggiore. The Façade.

S. Fermo Maggiore. The Apses

S. Fermo Maggiore.
Turone:
Crucifixion with knights.

S. Fermo Maggiore. Interior.

Two long flights of steps lead to the two entrances, one in the façade and one in the side, by which one enters the vast rectangular interior with its wooden coffered 'ship's keel' ceiling. The side entrance is covered by a high, late-14th century porch.

The interior of S. Fermo is rich with frescoes which provide a «running commentary» of Veronese painting from Turone to Pisanello, from approximately 1360 to 1430. The **Crucifixion with knights** is attributed to the former, while Pisanello executed the painted surround, and was perhaps responsible for the general plan, of the **Brenzoni monument** on the left wall. The fabric of the whole recalls the Serego monument in S. Anastasia. The sculptured part showing the Risen Christ flanked by angels with the sleeping soldiers at the foot of the sepulchre, is by a contemporary of Donatello, Nanni di Bartolo, called «il Rosso Fiorentino».

S. Fermo Maggiore.
Stefano da Verona, Choir of Angels.

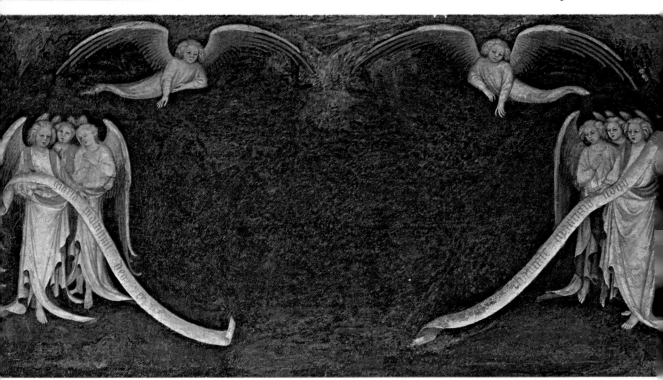

S. Fermo Maggiore. Martino da Verona, frescoes surrounding the pulpit.

Outside the draped curtains held up by two winged putti Pisanello painted the Annunciation, where his affinities with the art of Gentile da Fabriano may be clearly seen. Around the sculpted figure of God-the-Father above he also painted a series of airy baldachins beneath which, and to the sides, recent restoration work has revealed two Archangels. The painting surrounding the pulpit on the right wall, built by Barnaba Morano in 1396, is by Martino da Verona. The **Choir of Angels,** a fresco transferred onto canvas in 1958, is by Stefano da Verona (see his «Madonna of the Rosery» in the Castelvecchio Museum). Originally there was to be a painted Risen Christ in the centre, which Stefano did not execute because a sculpted figure was chosen instead. This fresco represents the Lombard period of the painter's artistic experience, just as the «Madonna of the Rosery» represents a period of transalpine influence. On the right at this point is the Brenzoni Chapel, which houses the tomb of Barnaba Morano, executed around 1411 by the sculptor Antonio da Mestre, and following the chapel is the tomb of Torello Saraina, author of the first printed work on the antiquities of Verona. It is in the form of an urn in red marble supported by two «torelli» (young bulls), a clear allusion to his name. The altar which follows, dedicated to the Trinity, was erected at his expense in 1523 and is a very early example of Classicism in Verona, previous to the activities and influence of Sanmicheli. The altarpiece is by Francesco Torbido, a Veronese painter of the school of Giorgione noted for his fine portraits. Arriving thus at the transept, we see at the end of the right arm the **Alighieri Chapel** which brings together the last of the Poet's descendents, the «doctor in Greek and Latin Messer Pietro», the doctor of law Lodovico and the canon Francesco, who erected the monument as directed in his brothers' wills, beginning in 1547. Its façade reproduces that of the Arco dei Gavi. The architect of the monument is unknown, although it is suggested that it was Francesco himself, an avid student of Vitruvius, whose work he

S. Fermo Maggiore, interior of the lower church.

prepared for a printed edition which however was never published; others attribute the work to Sanmicheli. The second chapel to the right of the main chapel contains the sculptural group of the «Mourning over the dead Christ», eight figures carved in tufa, two-thirds lifesize, of the mid 14th century. The presbytery is enclosed by an Ionic order choir screen built in 1573 in imitation of the one in the Duomo.

The left arm of the transept contains frescoes of the 14th century with scenes from the life of St. Francis, and at the end is a small enclosed space which houses the **funeral monument of the Torriani.** This was commissioned by the brothers Giambattista and Giulio dalla Torre in memory of their father Giulio (d. 1506) and brother Marcantonio (d. 1512), both professors of medicine in Padua, from the Paduan sculptor Andrea Briosco, called Riccio. The bronze reliefs on the sides of the sarcophagus are copies, the originals having remained in the Louvre after their removal there by the French in 1797. The Dalla Torre family was one of the foremost cultural forces in Verona at the beginning of the 16th century. Further on is the Chapel of the Immaculate Conception with its central altarpice of the Madonna and Child with St. Anne and four saints below, a solidly constructed work by G.F. Caroto datable to 1528. To the left is a public testimony to the horrors of the scourge of the plague of 1630, in the painting by Antonio Giarola, called Cavalier Coppa, showing «Verona imploring liberation from the plague», painted in 1636.

LOWER CHURCH, FRESCO

The lower church of S. Fermo, reached through a small door at the side of the porch on the left flank of the church, today serves as a «winter church». Its plan is very similar to that of S. Lorenzo, divided into three naves with apses and a transept with two apses facing in the same direction as those of the naves. The main apse has columns and two Ionic capitals of the Roman period incorporated into its fabric, which were taken as classical models in the early years of the 16th century. Several of the pilasters of the lower church still bear their original fresco decoration, including an «Annunciation» of the middle of the 12th century.

PORTA LEONI

Porta Leoni.

This name, which goes back at least to the 15th century, indicates the remains of two Roman gates, one of the Republican and one of the Claudian age, which back onto the corner house between Corticella Leoni and Via Leoni. The name is derived from a funeral fastigium in stone bearing two lions side by side, which is now behind the monument to king Humbert I. The Republican gate, of which only half of the internal face remains, rises half a metre behind the Imperial and it is thanks to this expedient that today we still have, on the older gate, what may be considered the «act of birth» of Verona as a city organised according to the criteria of Roman city planning. This is an inscription engraved upon what was the central pilaster, partially identified in the 16th century but not fully revealed and understood until 1959. The words of the inscription inform us that Publius Valerius, Quintus Cecilius, Quintus Servilius and Publius Cornelius, as a quadrumvirate and by decree of the decurions (city council), gave contracts for the building of the walls, gates and cloacae, and that the first two later approved the work. The Republican gate is for the most part built in brick, with the edges, friezes and cornices, and the inscription plaque, in tufa. We must imagine it with two apertures, 5,25 metres high and 3,30 wide, with two orders of six windows each above them. Roadworks have recently (1975) brought to light part of the façade facing away from the city, with foundations of one of the sixteen-sided towers flanking it. All this part is built in brick. About one century after their construction the two city gates were embellished and renovated, at least on their internal and external faces, so as to give them a more monumental aspect in keeping with Verona's elevated status of Augustan Colony, as opposed to her former rank as municipal city.

The remains of both these city gates provides us with the opportunity to compare the Republican and the Imperial; the first in brick and tufa with its precise and severe linearity; and the later superimposed gate in white Veronese stone, with a more complex and varied structure. Below were two apertures (only one has survived), each framed by fluted half columns with Composite capitals supporting an entablature with inscriptions on the architrave and a rather cramped pediment. The inscription, which is incomplete, cites one Tiberius Flavius Noricus, the son of Publius, member of the quadrumvirate. If we are to deduce that like the former gate, this bore the names of the ruling four, these must have been distributed above the internal and external arches of the apertures. Above the decorated pediment was a row of six windows, of which three remain, repeating the motif of the older gate. Radically different, however, was the third order with its high screen, which had no apertures and yet was imbued with a sense of movement by four freestanding spiral columns and a large central niche. Giovanni Caroto imagined this space adorned with a series of statues. The particular structural «animation» of this monument places it, together with Porta Borsari, as one of the first examples of the so-called Roman «Baroque».

Archeological remains.

Interior of «Juliet's Tomb».

JULIET'S TOMB

Tradition has it that Juliet is buried in the church of S. Francesco al Corso. In 1938 the sarcophagus long venerated by those who felt the need to substantiate their reverence for poetry in history was placed in the evocative half-shadows of the crypt. More recently the church was enriched in cultural content by its arrangement as an «Auditorium» and the opening of a new museum named for G.B. Cavalcaselle, for the exhibition of frescoes. Inaugurated in 1970, the museum houses a collection of Roman amphoras brought to light during excavations in the basements, and presents particularly those frescoes which had been removed from their original positions and awaited a more fitting exhibition space. First there are the frescoes from the 2nd level of the Grotto of SS. Nazaro e Celso, dated to approximately 1180, followed by those of the school of Giotto, painted in the early 14th century, from the church of Corte Lepia, near Vago (Verona). The fresco by Francesco Torbido, dominated by the figure of a warrior in classical armour, is from the house of Antonello Saraina in Via Stella, while the large frieze (1550-1560) by Domenico Brusasorzi and Bernardino India is from the façade of the house of Fiorio della Seta at Ponte Navi, demolished during work on the Adige embankments in 1890-95. Of particular interest as a work of restoration is the **music chamber,** painted in 1560 by Paolo Farinati for the Guarienti ai Filippini house. The small room has been reconstructed in accordance with its original measurements, with the same spaces left for doors, windows and the large fireplace. Here the fresco decoration, transferred to canvas partly in the last century and partly in our own times, has created within the museum the atmosphere of the privileged space of an aristocratic house of the 16th century.

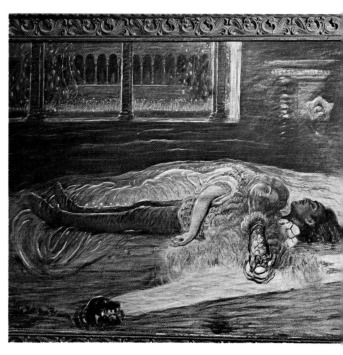

Juliet's Tomb. Angelo Dall'Oca Bianca, the two lovers united in death.

Juliet's Tomb. The cloister of S. Francesco al Corso.

Verona by night.

INDEX

PRINTED FOR:

Ditta Ivo ANCORA
Vicoletto Valle, 2/A
37100 VERONA
Tel. (045) 594069

Photography:
Falugi, Firenze - Ancora, Verona

Layout:
Storti Edizioni

Text:
Lanfranco Franzoni, Verona

Printed: February 1995